LEGITIMACY!

PAOLO DEALBERTI

Verkauft durch JEWIR - Germany

Copyright ©2012 Paolo Dealberti

1. Edition 2012
2. Edition 2015

ISBN-13: 978-1514756652

ISBN-10: 151475665X

"But when a long train of abuses and usurpation, pursuing invariably the same object, evinces a design to reduce them under absolute despotism is their right, it is their duty, to throw off such government and to provide new guards for their future security"

(Thomas Jefferson - The Declaration of Independence, 1776)

At the end ... what <u>we simply need</u> are **normal** people with an embrace of complexity to be able to understand what is complex.

To my best friends:

Paolo, Carlo, Shigenobu, Julius

Index

Appendices

Introduction

Legitimacy ...is a complex word for a complicate world.

Is our present collapsing and a new future is near to born?

Or is our future collapsed and our present crystallized in a status-quo?

Is It both and more? ...

The real problem is that we have lost the ability to generate visions.

We have managers but not leaders.

The economic elites think that is enough to read a lot of theory in an MBA.

The political elites are laser focused only to find electoral mechanisms and to bargains with the Not State Actors, (the global alternative powers),to survive.

In the middle a vacuum where the intellectual world finds itself lost in old words unable to describe the different form of modernity,(inside a network of 296 leading toWns), that can generate multiple futures.

Words are more than symbols because they are inner symbols and inside these articles I try to use such symbols to talk about geopolitics.

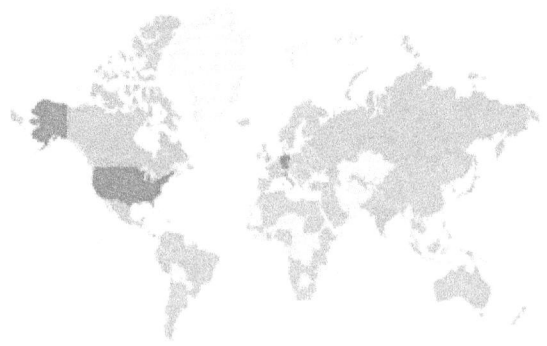

This small collection of articles was published inside Prosumerzen and Westphalia XXI in the period 2011-2012. Prosumerzen, Westphalia XXI ARE NET-ZINES both now inside the innovative Integrated Internet Cross-media Platform "Prosumerzen´s Diary of the World" :We achieved this success in Internet without any SEO and using an invented word. The map shows our worldwide audiences ,(around 30 millions visitors),in 23 languages.

Invented words?

Prosumerzen = **PRO**ducer + con**SUMER**+ citi**ZEN**

and Humpolitics = **HUM**an -geo**POLITICS**

Paolo Dealberti, Eching 2-12-2012

(2015: Prosumerzen and Westphalia XXI do not exist anymore and you can follow me at www.apperalpower.com)

...

Legitimacy

...

You can create the future…now. You need only 1 word!

June 16, 2011

We need words to…**but before to start this article I must thank the Futurist Thomas Frey** because I was inspired by one of his articles for the approach I will use inside this article

Words are inner symbols.

Personally the most terrific thing that I have found in Orwell´s 1984 was that in each new edition of the dictionary words were deleted …and if you have not words…how can you express ideas?

I speak four languages and I am studying my fifth and I know how is frustrating to have ideas, (in your language), but not being able to express them in another because you do not know the right words.

Once King Carl V told that you are how many languages you speak.

Words, we told words and the problem is that if you do not have a word to express an idea you cannot show/explain a vision.

Then we can think to a solution in a world that desperately needs new words!

The future is never only one and History has not a linear trend.

We have the choice to create the future we want starting from our past because the only and real tradition is that anything,(someday),changes and the only evolution is inside the tradition.

I firmly believe that a **revolution has only a retroactive value. This because the day we see a revolution to achieve its goals this "simply and only" means that something that yesterday was an exception today is the NEW rule.**

Let´s take internet. Internet can be also a thermometer of the souls and the emotions in the web.

How? Again, if we listen and use words…. If we measure the most used words this analytic tells us what the world is feeling and thinking if not dreaming.

Starting from this idea we can realize that we are able to create words that will originate emotions till someone will feel the need to realize them.

That day these worlds will be less revolutionary and a lot more part of our daily life but that day someone will start to do something… And this something will be not a revolution but only and simply the new "tradition", (of course till the next revolution and then…).

And this is the solution!

We need words to create the future in the present: this is our challenge. In other words to create one of the possible future and to achieve it NOW!

How?

Step 1: we need words.

They need to describe an idea. And this idea MUST break the paradigms!

If you not find words, you must invent them.

Let´s take, for example, an invented word like Prosumerzen that synthesizes a concept:

PROducer + con**SUMER** + citi**ZEN** = PROSUMERZEN

This concept explains an ethic approach where happiness is at the center and we achieve it inside our normal life doing normal things.

When we produce,(PROducers), something we must respect our environment. That is the place where we want to live as citiZEN. Then, and at the same time, we must also respect the community. How? Being honest in the same way we expect from others when we are conSUMER and we buy their products.

When we consume,(conSUMERs),we have to be responsible. The same responsibility we ask to the PROducers and that we want to have from the citiZENs of our towns. If not we will kill this wonderful but fragile world.

When we are citiZENs: we must be responsible for our and for the next generation. And this means a harmonic balance between our **SPIRIT**ual and mat**ERIAL**, (**SPIRITERIAL**, again a new word…), life. And to be "Spiriterial" means to be able to achieve a sustainable balance that forces us to be,(both),a responsible PROducer and conSUMER.

For example, let´s look at the energy of the Jasmine Revolution in North Africa and in the Middle East…of the 15-M Movimiento in Spain and of the Referendum in Italy…all started with some words and then…

Which word? Why not Prosumerzen or Spiriterial …for example…

Step 2: let´s buildup ideas and then visions

Once that you have a word you have to use it like a brick to build ideas and visions. To create bridges, bonds instead of walls.

And all can help you.

Short or long stories, storyboards, graphic art, animations, models, surveys, interviews, videos **…anything we can catch if we smelt the "scent of the streets"** !!! In a world where you can broadcast a decent video with a 70€ camcorder …all and more is possible, is it? YES IT IS!!! If we want that.!

Step 3: let´s share it in a network

To Share …to share and again to share. Let´s share!!!

Then each person that will start to use this word will be a brick to build this pacific and harmonic **evolution**.

The more people use this word the more and faster it will be part of our life and then of our desires, hopes, visions.

This means to be part of our vision of our future and it will be a future that we start to choose and to create now.

The network will metabolize the ideas and visions and, more important, will start to evolve creating its own.

Step 4: the vision reaches the world

At that point the vision starts to reach the world.

W. Shakespeare wrote "you know the world but the world does not know you".

Now it is time that the world knows you and then also the (new) words you believe to be able to shape the world.

Logically this is the most delicate moment because the word starts to be self-perpetuating and to be "less revolutionary" as well as more part of the "daily life", of if you prefer to be part of us, than to be the "fuel" of a revolution.

To embody an evolution that lasts and not a revolution that burns.

Step 5:… let's listen to the trend

See the word and the visions to growth… search them in the net because **you belong to the net as well as to the physical world.**

Our reality is a DUAL composed by the daily mix of physical and digital life we live and that is our routine,

The world needs hope and the future is now.

Words are inner symbols

Please find your word and start to inspire us!

Humpolitics

June 22, 2011

The Bilan Geostrategique 2010, published by Le Monde / International Institute of Strategic Studies starts by saying that every age has its theory that explains everything and then there are the geopolitical trends of the moment. I

t seems that we live in a world where trends become theories and theories become so fashionable to be considered reals.

On average around every year the world seems to face the final crisis and all remixes

It seems... If we consider the short time between 1987 and 2011 we can find 21 so called "epochal" crisis:

1987 stock market crisis in October
1990 implosion of Japan
1994 / 5 Mexican debt crisis
1997 Asian financial crisis
1998 Russian debt crisis
1998 collapse of hedge fund TLCM
1999 Brazilian debt crisis
1999 NATO war against Yugoslavia, which provides
humanitarian armed intervention as limiting the sovereignty
of a Nation
1999 Millennium Bug
2000 stock market crash of Web 1.0
2001 ...9/11
2001 debt crisis in Turkey and Argentina

2001 war in Afghanistan
2003 War in Iraq
2003 an horrific hot summer with fires and thousands deaths from the hot. The media starts to talk about the end of the world on the environmental causes
2006 Pandemia 1
2008 9/15 and the U.S. financial crisis
2009 Pandemia 2
2009 financial crisis
2010, China has its first trade deficit and begin to talk about a" post-China world" ... by the way without ever created the "China controlled world"
2010 Jasmine Revolution

If on average around every year the world rewrites itself something does not work.

Maybe we have lost the sense of balance. Do we have?

The sense of balance is the key.

We describe it as HUMPOLITICS. A word invented by us (**HUM**an-geo**POLITICS**), to describe a dimension that contains geopolitics and humanity operating on medium and long time.

It means to go to smell the humanity inside our streets.

Streets? Our streets are borders, limes, where the so called fault lines are located. We can describe them like some kind of "**Border-lands**" because our geo-political developments have a social, cultural, historical origin before than a geographical one.

We believe that are more important the human generated mutations than the constraints of mountains and rivers.

Mutations that result inside our towns',(by the way towns are always the "virtual world" by excellence where we have been building real symbols, timeliness and places that we describe as society). And our towns are connected to each other but not from itineraries ranging from directions in a dynamic grid where each place has its own hierarchy. A network composed by 296 leading towns that are so cool to shape the different and equivalent forms of our modernity,(see Appendix 3). Inside such Border-lands there is the intersection between geography and politics, and here, more than in other places, the life is characterized on where you live. And so it could happen that in the Balkan in the twenty-first,(where there is a talk of ethnic divisions of a territory originated in the twelfth),they think that the future, the solution to that division is to be part of the EU. In the Balkan ,like all over in the world, does not the persistence of nations or empires that matters but that of political forms in which people, who live there, give substance to their believe using what they know. Our legends tell about us more than statistics or reports. This because legends, poetry, history speak of the layers that are stacked in the collective consciousness created by common events when a report issued by a qualified institution has to say something that, ultimately, not too much mind to those who have financed it. Our travels to our Border-lands are talking about statistics and events analyzed in the light of words, legends and poems. This because the objective reality it is not what we know but what we believe... and the world is based on mental maps. Always and only the human dimension is what shapes the world. That is how our beliefs take the forms, (among the possible ones), we choose given our knowledge. We'll talk of the rites of passage of the forces that generate the different but synergic forms of power,(hard, soft, smart, appeal and leverage, see Appendix 1). Of the men who make them and their humanity that push them to this.

Our happiness is a geo-politic key-factor!

April 19, 2011

The **Gross National Happiness**, (GNH), index is an indicator that measures our quality of life or social progress in more holistic and psychological terms than the Gross Domestic Product, (GDP).

It is not something new and we have to back to 1972 and to thank the Bhutan's former King Jigme Singye Wangchuck.

He introduced the GNH to magnify Bhutan's commitment to building an economy that would realize a culture based on Buddhist spiritual values.

The Centre for Bhutan Studies under the leadership of Professor Karma Uraand and Professor Michael Pennock has developed a sophisticated survey instrument to measure the population's general level of well-being.

In two years of work was created the **Gross National Happiness, (GNH) ,** index,(I) .

The revolutionary dimension of this index is that the HARMONIC and SUSTAINABLE development of a society takes place when there is MATERIAL AND SPIRITUAL empowerment /development. Both developments,(spiritual and material), must be side by side to mutually and synergic complement and reinforce.

It must be SPIRITERIAL.

This is possible if 4 pillars are achieved:

1) the promotion of a sustainable development
2) the preservation and promotion of cultural values

3) the conservation of the natural environment
4) the establishment of good governance,(social environment)

In other terms: economy, culture, environment, rule of law are one thing and only as a "synergic whole" can support our harmonic development.

This index is a powerful geo-political tool and it is **TRANS-CULTURAL**.

Thanks to the GNH the happiness of the citizens becomes a geo-political key variable to keep into account and it is based on the following 7 measurable factors:

1. **Economic Wellness**: Indicated via direct survey and statistical measurement of economic metrics such as consumer debt, average income to consumer price index ratio and income distribution

2. **Environmental Wellness**: Indicated via direct survey and statistical measurement of environmental metrics such as pollution, noise and traffic

3. **Physical Wellness**: Indicated via statistical measurement of physical health metrics such as severe illnesses

4. **Mental Wellness**: Indicated via direct survey and statistical measurement of mental health metrics such as usage of antidepressants and rise or decline of psychotherapy patients

5. **Workplace Wellness**: Indicated via direct survey and statistical measurement of labor metrics such as jobless claims, job change, workplace complaints and lawsuits

6. **Social Wellness**: Indicated via direct survey and statistical measurement of social metrics such as discrimination, safety, divorce rates, complaints of domestic conflicts and family lawsuits, public lawsuits, crime rates

7. **Political Wellness**: Indicated via direct survey and statistical measurement of political metrics such as the quality of local democracy, individual freedom, and foreign conflicts.

Around two years ago Paris proposed to consider the GHN to measure the condition of the French people. President Sarkozy was responding to recommendations made by two Nobel economists, Joseph Stiglitz and Amartya Sen. The two economists called on world leaders to move away from a purely economic concept of gross domestic product, which measures economic production, to wellbeing and sustainability suggesting a shift from production to greater attention to household wealth and an assessment of whether countries were growing sustainably or damaging the environment.

A lot of skepticism if not irony raised but also the Premier Cameron was interested on that and thanks to this decision London is among the first government to do it. The UK government will start measuring people's psychological and environmental wellbeing using a GNH Index: 25 -11-2010 was an historical date because it was asked to the independent national statistician Jil Matheson to devise questions to add to the existing household survey by as early as next spring, (2011).

2001 will be the first year for this survey and the new data will be placed alongside existing measures to create a bundle of indications about quality of life in the UK and the data results could be published quarterly.

This is a revolutionary step that will affect not only the internal life of countries like Bhutan, France, Canada ,(even if not part of the official data set), or the UK but all the world.

Someone can call it "soft power" others can describe it as "social competitive model able to create a consensus around a country" and it is both and for this it is **an extremely interesting new element, (if not the most interesting), in the last decades we can use to describe a country and to judge a government.**

The GNH can shape our vision of the world and change the ranking of the variable we usually consider to judge a country inside the international geo-politics and geo-economics scenario.

If we consider the GNH it has not so much value that you have more than 9.5 % GDP growth pro year when the pollution of your towns is so high that since almost ten years it is almost impossible to take a picture with a satellite... for example in Shanghai or Beijing.

Or it has less value that your army has the most sophisticated weaponry of the world, (in some case two or three generations ahead other countries), when in your secondary schools you need a metal detector to make them a safe place... for example in the USA.

And it has not so much value that you create an artificial "town of science" if some of the inhabitants cannot be free to enjoy their religious belief or to kiss each other in public ... for example like in the KSA.

Or maybe it is not so important that your central bank is so able to control inflation when in your continent the word "assimilation" means failure…for example like in the EU.

This is a mental and cultural tsunami but a positive one.

The day we start to consider that people are before and beyond statistics is the day we empower.

Note   :
(i) http://grossnationalhappiness.com/

The World middle-class:how a self-fuelling "myth" could be used by someone to affect our democracies

September 26, 2011

We have mentioned how populism and diplomatic arrogance have manipulated the true about the Greek debt,(I),and how three parallel but interconnected crisis in the EU,USA and China are the battle ground of a strong confrontation between the elites of the SA´s and the NSA´s ,(II).

We mention again the disclaimer of the S&P report that has downgraded the Italian ratings:

"Ratings Information and Data Policy but does not guarantee the accuracy, adequacy, or completeness of any information used."

And we finished with the following question: "Should you believe a report with such conclusion?"

On clear terms how can you take a decision using a report that tells you that it does not guarantee the accuracy, adequacy, or completeness of any information used. No one can do it but is seems that this is enough to LEGITTIMATE the financial speculation. This is the key. The elected elites are so de-legitimate that even a report, (that ends telling that it is not sure about the data that contains), can be credible.

But to better understand how it is possible we need to talk

25

about one of the strongest economic myth of the last twenty years: the so-called world middle class.

The OECD published on January 2010 one of the most important academic documents to support this idea: "The emerging middle class in developing countries" by Homi Kharas.

This report esteems that the world middleclass is composed by around 1.8 billion people, (= the parameter are expenditures between 10USD-100USD/day):

- 664 million in Europe, (450 in the EU)
- 525 million in Asia, (125 in Japan)
- 338 million in North America (230 in the USA, the biggest concentration among individual countries)
- 32 million in sub-Saharan Africa

According to this report a country like Russia -without any industrial backbone and with an export based only on gas and oil,(we remind that Russia exports oil and gas but imports gasoline due the lack of refineries)-can be richer than a developed country with the biggest industrial structure in the EU like Germany.

Computer based forecasting is one thing common sense and historical knowledge are another but this incredible data introduces us about the credibility of all. But we back later about this point and we continue to mention data of the OECD report that used like a Bible by the believers of this economic dogma.

This report forecasts some scenarios and in order to achieve this goal it explains that "we do not have the expertise to seriously review all 145 countries so some quantitative shortcut method is inevitable, (ibidem page 19)."

It is interesting to evaluate these "quantitative shortcuts" and how they (dramatically) affect the whole picture.

I) 4 groups of countries

    a) Affluent, advanced economies with rather low rates of technological progress.
    b) Converging developing economies closing the income gap with the USA.
    c) Stalled, middle income developing economies with no convergence model, (in other terms these countries prisoners in the middle income trap).
    d) Poor, low income developing economies with no convergence trends.

For example Mexico and Brazil, (with their diversified economies and preferential) seems to be caught in the middle income trap when Russia, (with its commodity based economy), seems to be a fast growing emerges A nice and interesting example of "some quantitative shortcut method is inevitable" is it?

II) The technological advance is only 1.3% per year and that mean that IT does not effect the convergence.

In an internet –and-high tech-based world again another interesting example of "some quantitative shortcut method is inevitable" is it? Yes, it is a quantities shortcut method full of dramatic consequences inside the "Internet of Things".

III) The capital accumulation is maintained at historical rate

If we consider that the historical trend is 1807-2006 we have to assume that China or India will have less than 1% increase. Again another interesting example of "some quantitative shortcut method is inevitable" is it? Yes it is, but unlucky inside a computer simulation could be "inevitable" but inside the real world it can only generate some dramatic misunderstandings.

IV) Constant labor participation rates in each country

This "simply" forgets how demography can affect a country. For example Russia simply cannot maintain a constant labor participation rates because it is reducing its population. Or the USA will have a better flow of young immigrants than the EU that due to its aging population cannot maintain it. But also China, that on 2030 will be older than the USA, cannot maintain it. By the way, the Chinese leadership since years is telling that China will become old before to become rich.

In other words: China will become old before to become rich.

Additionally this approach "simply" forgets that the productivity can increase or reduce and to be constant in relative term must be reduced.

And last but not least it does not consider that the technology will increase our working time. And this means that we must be able to manage intern-generational problems.

Again another interesting example of "some quantitative shortcut method is inevitable" is it? Yes of course but only inside a computer simulation and never inside the geopolitical world.

V) Too easy access to credit

We have told that China is ranked 61st inside the World Bank´ Doing Business Survey and that means that less than half of Chinese SMEs have a bank loan.

Unlucky it is not possible to appreciate the value of this data if we forget that in 2007 started a reform of the banking system aimed to minimize the non-performing loans and that despite it on 2010 the liabilities of the banks raised at 150%. It we consider the two data they simply and dramatically show that more than half of the SMEs will never have a loan!

To avoid considering it was a "quantitative shortcut" that hided a different picture about the future sustainability of a Chinese growth based on the internal consumer demand able to replace the export leaded expansion...

We appreciate Dr.Kharas ´ competence and amazing intellectual honesty admitting the shortcuts used in the report. And we wonder how it was possible the too many did not consider that these shortcuts reduced the effectiveness of the forecasts.

This report can be used as an interesting theoretical exercise about possible trends but its intrinsic admitted limits in term of accuracy cannot make it as a reference for political decisions.

As Dr. Kharas mention in his "The New global middle class a cross-over from west to east" there is "a danger that China´s economy could stall before the middle class matures"

Despite all this inaccuracy too many are considering credible that this will be the trend of the middle class

2011 : 1.8 billion people
2020 : 3.2 billion people
2030 : 4.9 billion people

And around 85% of this growth will come from Asia. In the USA the vertical social mobility will generate a constant trend for the middle class. In Europe it will rise but the demographic decline will reduce the relative amount.

What is the risk with this over-estimation of the worldwide middleclass?

The risk is the creation and diffusion of a common belief able to self-fulfilling a vision about markets that will always growth. At least "somewhere" around the world and this "somewhere" will be the land where the profits will be made.

This belief can be a danger for our democracies when too many multinationals, (NSA´s), believe, (as they believe), that it does not matter too much if the situation in the west will be worse because they will always find a market. And thanks to this market it will possible to generate profits that will protect the value of shares, (and by the way not mention that it will be possible to get "virtual" inside the financial markets and offshore locations).

In other terms: why a board of directors should be concerned about the social consequences of industrial relocation,(and related cut of jobs),from the country Alpha to Beta or Gamma? They are not concerned about that till:

a) The new workers in Beta and Gamma will replace those in Alpha as market
b) They can gain and get virtual inside offshore locations as well as the financial markets
c) They can live in armored gate communities or down town buildings
d) They can lobby our not competent,(elected as well not elected),political elites as well as our easy to manipulate technocracies and bureaucracies.

But unlucky the consequence of this reduced global social, (if not political), responsibility will generate a situation where the reduced living conditions will give support to the rise of extremism and populism and hate with nations ,(see the current euro-crisis),as well as between social classes. This trend will find alleys also in the part of the elected elite, (not only in extremists parties), of the technocracy as well as of the bureaucracy that think to benefit from this situation. The "revolving doors" inside such 3 worlds are working well.

We want a world with less and less poverty but at same time we want also a world that faces a sustainable development and this development can be sustainable only and only if it is not the "tool" to create a less free world.

Notes

I)   http://prosumerzen.net/2011/09/22/from-populism-to-a-crisis-of-legitimacy-by-paolo-dealberti/

II)   http://prosumerzen.net/2011/09/21/chancellor-merkel-co-crisis-of-legitimacy-by-paolo-dealberti/

The 3 overlapping crisis: China, EU, USA

October 17, 2011

1- The world today

We are living in a formal state of anarchy that lasts since the beginning of history and that makes this state a natural geopolitical condition. During centuries variables like the different form of governments, the influx of the church,(since the Pharaohs to the modern times),and the geographical distance have generated different solutions to this problems. In the II AC four empires had the control of the Euro-Asia landscape. Today we have a so called "a-polar" world with a GX structure. We prefer to use GX instead of G8/G20 because inside this formal state of anarchy we have different "G" according to the dimension we are considering. For example when we talk about international finance we have a G23,(not G20 because we have to add three of the 32 different kinds of NSA´s,(see Appendix 4), to the G20 and they are the IMF, the Financial Multinationals and the Ratings Agencies as Private Controller), and a G5 when we talk about the UN or a G7 when we talk of the international organized crime and so on.

Inside this framework since 2008 we are living (also) the latest episode of the contrast between states and Not State Actors/NSA´s,(or sub national powers).

An interesting dimension is that affecting the political elites, (elected and not), inside the three most important geopolitical entities in the world:the USA, the EU and China.

In Europe we have three levels of (conflicting) elected political elites, (regional, national and European), plus 3 NSA´s controlled by State Actors,(SA´s):the EU, the European Central Bank and the NATO.

In the USA the elected political elite, (Congress and Senate), is facing the most important elected officer in the world, the President.

In China the political elite in Beijing is elected by the Communist Party the represents the last evolution of the oldest bureaucratic culture in the world, (born in the II BC).

2-The USA: 2011 or?

We start with the USA.

"In the USA the familiar litany of the irreversible decline has found application in higher interest rates, low savings rates and mounting government deficits. Industrial productivity and the investment that might have accelerated it lagged. American business did not organize itself for exports. Pressured by new financial criteria and a freshly minded generation of CFO, industry aimed at short term profits to raise the stock price. It horizons dipped from five years to a quarter it is not a surprise if investments lagged or were deferred "simply" because it would not result in an immediate profit or balance sheet. American competitors had not such restraint. As a result two generations of Americans reveled in excessive consumption while competitors saved and invested. The American grasshopper was increasingly bested by Japanese and Europeans ants. This problem was not doubt exacerbated by American´s own unwillingness to allow their government to save, even if they would not. The government´s failure to save had much to do with continuing 200 to 300 billion $ defense budgets: it was not only social program that broke the USA. Nuclear deterrence, more than

40 allies to support and spending on conventional weaponry represented high opportunity costs for the continuing progress and prosperity of the American economy .But prosperity for US allies was sometimes bought at the expense of economic progress at home".

Nothing new ? It seems but these words were wrote not on 2011, even not on 2008 or on 2001 but on 1992 by a commission of the Senate.

We do not totally agree on that vision about the "Washington's altruism" because:

1) The mentioned investments generated Made in USA exports

2) The investments in the defense were mostly in the USA. Either to pay the soldiers,(they can combat anywhere in the world but they use their incomes to buy in America),or to pay the weaponry produced by American companies in the USA. Companies that pay taxes, generate incomes to finance R&D and to raise workers. This is all and exclusively a benefit for the USA long before of that one for the helped countries.

But also "it was the strength of the ... consensus that explains why Americans readily consented to the establishment of institutions and governing practices previously identified with despotic governments. The establishment, in peace time, of standing military forces more powerful than those of any nation on hearth,the creation of intelligence agencies charged not only with assessing threats but also conducting covert operations; the claim of authority by the Presidency to employ American military forces on short notice and without congressional consent –all this would have been looked upon by the Founding Fathers as incompatible with maintenance at home of free institutions. Yet enemies learn one another's weapons as indeed they must. For a state with the political traditions for the USA , such institutions and doctrine might be justified only on the grounds of manifest necessity , as a regrettable yet inescapable departure from norms and practices we wished to maintain but could not... but that they even came to be seen as part of the natural order of things" Words that we are used to hear after 9/11 because of the intrusion in the private life of the Americans but wrote in 1992, (IV David C. Hendrickson The renovation of American foreign policy FA Vol. 71/2 1992).And the consensus was also in that case against an external enemy, (in this case not Bin Laden but the billion times more dangerous USSR).

And also Thomas Jefferson warned that one potent source of corruption was the relationship seen to exist between war and public debts. In other words we could tell " In the United States there is palpable revulsion against further international heroics, not because of failure abroad ,as with the case with Vietnam, but because domestic priorities have been so chronically underserved. Homeless people are beginning to populate even suburban streets ; the twin problems of crime and drugs have yet to be solved ;American education remain ineffective ,despite large expenditures. Infrastructure, inner-cities and family solidarity have eroded under the treble impact of luxurious private consumption, foreign imports and a reversal of public spending priorities. And the recession continues. Fiscal policy is stymied – the government cannot afford to spend more because of its heavily indebted international and domestic position"

Again words that we are used to hear every day on 2011 but they were wrote on 1992. Words used to comment a situation that lasts almost since the mid ´80´s and wrote just after a victorious war without consequences for the USA like that against Iraq to free Kuwait.

And it is logic that "America yearns for a statesman who can set nation back on a progressive economic track. When that happens,as it eventually must, national security spending will be rationed to a small fraction of its present massive dosage. The temptation to put American domestic priorities first may well become overwhelming, as it did in the 1920´s. It may be accompanied by a disastrous re-focusing on the American umbilicus."

Again …1992 and that days President Bush Sr. started the first 50 billion $ defense cut … .

But the USA will face the risk of a challenger able to become the inspiration for an alternative consensus because the prospective reanimation of ideological conflict cannot be dismisses either. A real Smart Power player.

"The most potent future antagonism the world could witness is a radical division between the USA and the rest of the world. The westernization of modern world is as yet incomplete. Beneath the external policy of a trading state boil nationalist resentments direct to a half century of American tutelage and Western neglect. nationalism and militarism are bubbling up against , contempt for an economically inept America resonates throughout culture and institutions. … that ,while having achieved economic equality or superiority ,they are sill relegated to second or third place politically. Such US politics may lead to seek the independent military and strategic strength need to establish a new political identity. A nuclear deterrent would be directed against no one ,but it could be designed to earn the respect and attention. If current trends continue it may not be too long before ideological rationalizations of Confucian strength and vitality are propounded by OMISSIS as antidotes to supposed Western decadence and lethargy. A vocation in South East Asia might again become tempting as economic conflict with the US intensifies. Burgeoning economic ties in the Asian-Pacific region might tempt to forge another co-prosperity sphere. The economic influence would be stretched int a form of political tutelage or even imperialism. Such policy becomes the most credible if partially masked by financial and economic controls that merely induce dependents parties to yield resources and territorial demands. The US, once, ruled Latina America through its own dollar diplomacy ".

China 2011 ? Not at all Japan 1992 short before the boom of the speculative bubble that relegated Japan in to a 19 years deflationary spiral. And today the internal liabilities of the Chinese banking system have reached 150% and less then 50% of the SME´s can reach the needed credit. Only to remember it. It is clear that isolation of key participants, (and the USA is the most important), could pave the way for a renaissance of expansionist ambitions in other quarter of the globe. If not managed in a proper way isolationism, ideology and pacification could erode the existing structure of the "great concert" and the USA are the key player both as SA and because the NSA´s,(multinationals, media outlet, NGO´s, private security forces, financial powerhouse and so on...), that hub there.And before that we focus on the USA we must remember that the threat of a collapse of the international economy,(trading),will be the :

- mortal check for the progress of China ,despite its trillions of reserves in US dollars. If someone needs an historical analogy ,please, keep in mind that China today is more dependent by exports then Victorian Britain in 1840.

- The USA cannot pull out of the recession till the world slumps

- The EU is even more dependent than the USA. For example Germany with the adoption of "Agenda 2010" has renounced to have an internal demand to be able to keep labor costs of a non-competitive labor force under control and be able to export.

Historia magistra vitae tells us that markets must keep open but the 1930´s and the Great Depression of 1873 tell other. It will better for the populism in Paris and Berlin to remember the economic crisis in 1873 if they think that a strong EU, (that time division was among economic blocks based on the colonies),can be the "market of last resort".

As the UK and later the USA learnt also China must learn to become a mature creditor. A mature creditor is a creditor able to increasingly concede a balance surplus in its own market to borrowers and recipients of its investments, (in this case the WSF ones). But this cannot take place if the imbalance between the USA and China is not re-dressed ,(as it was that between the USA and Japan in the ´90´s).

It seems that the 3-level strategy behind the worldwide campaign of FDI and buying of bonds by Beijing can help to achieve it.

This 3-level strategy ,unlucky, is unnoticed both in its complexity and in its long term consequences because all are ,(short minded),focused on the same useless rhetoric about the US/West decline used when ,for example, the Japanese bought the Plaza Center in New York.

The strategy is structured as follow

I) When China buys bonds and companies Beijing buys market share in each country of investment. The citizens of the countries where they buy can use the money that they do not use to buy the bonds issued by their governments to buy products,(also Made in China or with Made in China components). In a few words. If we have 100$ of bonds or share available in to the market and they are bought by China the US citizens can use this amount of money to buy products and among them also Made in China And because the US Citizens can use this money to buy products instead of bonds/shares the US economy will grow. And because is growing will be more and more the safer place to invest,(= read to buy bonds and shares). And because bonds are wanted their interests,(the cost for the issuer), is decreasing. But also because the market is growing it will be easier to fund American companies and this money will be used for R&D to boost the American technology supremacy,(please never forget that the whole world has a commercial deficit with the USA when we talk about hi-tech...). But even investors buy American shares and bonds they will hold American assets in American dollar and they were the less interested on the "failure" of the USA. Then the so-called deficit is an imperial cost that the world pays to have a market and stability.At the end of the day: who holds whom? The market,(the US citizen), or the buyer of bonds/share,(a Chinese one).

II)   If China uses a part of its reserves in dollars the value of the euro will growth and that of the dollar will fall. This will make the US export more competitive without affecting the yuan. The USA is the biggest Chinese markets and if they start to import this will be a benefit. Additionally this will reduce the American pressure to devaluate the Chinese currency.

III) In a middle-long term perspective Beijing is creating the premises to open its own market to products (also) produced by foreign companies owned by its capitals. That day millions of terabits will be spent to explain the "Chinese decline" but, at the end of the day, the revenues will flow to China. Like today almost 1/ 3 of the revenues for the Chinese export must be read with a different set of statistics because revenues for not Chinese companies!

A "Great Coalition" united by the common political interest to keep the markets open and growing is not doomed to fail.

Tomorrow we will talk about how the two "arrogant capitals, (Washington and New York),as dividing the country.(*)

Notes

1) About the NSA´s http://prosumerzen.net/category/from-geopolitics-to-biopsherepolitics/no-state-actors-nsa/

(II)   http://prosumerzen.net/2011/09/26/world-middle-class-how-a-self-fuelling-%e2%80%9cmyth%e2%80%9d-could-be-used-by-someone-to-affect-our-democracies/

Chancellor Merkel & Co. : A crisis of legitimacy

September 21, 2011

Chancellor Merkel started to be a bit populist on 15-10-2010 when at the national convention of the youth federation of her party, (CDU); he told that the foreigners were the problem that blocked Germany. The audience exploded in standing ovation. The German TV broadcasted this only once and the reason is a compressible embarrass in the term that it should be better if these words were not heard abroad. Historically the last time that a Chancellor blamed a social group to be the origin of the German problems was with Hitler.**We do not tell and firmly not believe that Chancellor Merkel is a far-right politician** but the reaction of the youths of the party is an interesting example of the national mood in Germany.

It was the period of the populist and racist best-seller by the, (at that time), Chairman of the German Central Bank Sarasin. He was fired by Chancellor Markel but his book was a bestseller that had more than 25 editions in four months. A racist as well ridiculous book where the statistics used to support the thesis contradict the author....It was the period where a survey showed that around 28% of the Germans wanted a far right policy against the foreigners. Patrick Gensing, (his investigative blog www.npd-blog.info received the Grimme Online Award), is writing since long time that the far right / neo-nazi party NPD in its documents and webs talks about the new "final solution" that means the deportation of 15.000.000 of foreigners. The NPD has elected in around 200 town councils and in the parliament of two lands. We wonder when the authority will put this party out of law. Do we have to wait till they use the word lager, (concentration camp), instead of deportierung, (deportation)?

In 2011 it was and it is also possible to hear university teachers tell to avoid to use "cloud computing services" supplied by Anglo-American world leader companies because it is not possible to trust them, (we wonder if some of them believe the theory of the global complot run by Hebrew and Masons... in this case it will be sad to see that qualified professors believe to something nice only for a Don Brown's novel).

Inside this social mood Chancellor Merkel and its party, (CDU), as well as the sister regional Bavarian party, (CSU), decided to turn populists.

At that point something happened and we describe it as the Greece debt- &- euro crisis.

It is now time to call things with their real name: a Euro-crisis to avoid the bankruptcy of MISMANAGED French and Germany top banks that supplied in an irresponsible way too much credit to Greece. If we describe it in this way, as it is and we supply data about it, we can stop both the speculation and the populism. Greece is a debtor because has found creditors.These creditors did not lend money to Greece to allow its people to have longer holidays or to retreat before than the Germans, (as someone told), but to give the chance to buy products and to build infrastructures/products Made in Germany and in France. It was not by coincidence sellers and creditors come from the same countries.

To be clear German and French bank lend billions euro to Athens to give to Greece the chance to pay infrastructures built by German and French companies. If you prefer Athens with the right hand received the money of the loans and with the left used the same money to pay its suppliers. Till Greece has been bought Made in France and Made in Germany it was a virtuous country engaged on the developing of its infrastructure…but one day they become the lazy people that abused of the euro. By coincidence that day was the day that German and French banks found to get short in liquidity. The EU-wide banking stress, (II), confirmed it ,(August 2011).

Table 1 Banks capital ratios without capital raising

Adverse scenario

	2010	2012	< 2%	< 3%	< 4%	< 5%	< 6%	< 7%	< 8%	< 9%	< 10%	> 10%
AT	8.2%	7.6%	0		0	1	0	1	1	0	0	0
BE	11.4%	10.2%	0		0	0	0	0	0	0	0	2
CY	7.7%	4.8%	0		1	0	1	0	0	0	0	0
DE	9.4%	6.8%	0		1	0	2	3	1	0		3
DK	9.8%	10.8%	0		0	0	0	0	0	1		3
ES	7.4%	6.5%	4		3	2	2	0	3	2		2
FI	12.2%	11.6%	0		0	0	0	0	0	0	0	1
FR	8.4%	7.5%	0		0	0	2	1	1	0	0	0
GB	10.1%	7.6%	0		0	0	1	2	1	0	0	0
GR	10.2%	5.7%	1		0		0	2	0	0	0	0
HU	12.3%	13.6%	0		0	0	0	0	0	0	0	1
IE	6.2%	-0.1%	2		1	0	0	0	0	0	0	0
IT	7.4%	6.5%	0		0	1	2	1	0	0	0	0
LU	12.0%	13.3%	0		0	0	0	0	0	0	0	1
MT	10.5%	10.4%	0		0	0	0	0	0	0	0	1
NL	10.6%	9.4%	0		0	0	0	1	0	1	1	1
NO	8.3%	9.0%	0		0	0	0	0	0	1	0	0
PL	11.8%	12.2%	0		0	0	0	0	0	0	0	1
PT	7.1%	5.2%	0		1	0	2	0	0	0	0	0
SE	9.0%	9.5%	0		0	0	0	0	1	2	1	
SI	5.7%	4.2%	0		1	0	0	0	0	0	0	0
Total	8.9%	7.4%	7	0	8	5	13	10	10	6		17

43

Table 2 Banks capital ratios with capital raising to 30th April 2011

Adverse scenario

	2010	2012	< 2%	< 3%	< 4%	< 5%	< 6%	< 7%	< 8%	< 9%	< 10%	> 10%
AT	8.2%	7.6%	0	0	0	1	0	0	1	1	0	0
BE	11.4%	10.2%	0	0	0	0	0	0	0	0	0	2
CY	7.7%	5.7%	0	0	0	0	1	1	0	0	0	0
DE	9.4%	6.8%	0	0	0	0	1	4	2	1	1	2
DK	9.8%	11.9%	0	0	0	0	0	0	0	0	1	3
ES	7.4%	7.3%	0	0	3	2	1	5	1	3	2	2
FI	12.2%	11.6%	0	0	0	0	0	0	0	0	0	1
FR	8.4%	7.5%	0	0	0	0	0	2	1	1	0	0
GB	10.1%	7.6%	0	0	0	0	0	1	2	1	0	0
GR	10.2%	6.1%	1	0	0	1	0	2	0	0	0	0
HU	12.3%	13.6%	0	0	0	0	0	0	0	0	0	1
IE	6.2%	9.8%	0	0	0	0	0	0	1	0	0	2
IT	7.4%	7.3%	0	0	0	0	2	1	1	0	0	0
LU	12.0%	13.3%	0	0	0	0	0	0	0	0	0	1
MT	10.5%	10.4%	0	0	0	0	0	0	0	0	0	1
NL	10.6%	9.4%	0	0	0	0	1	0	1	1	1	
NO	8.3%	9.0%	0	0	0	0	0	0	1	0	0	
PL	11.8%	12.2%	0	0	0	0	0	0	0	0	0	1
PT	7.1%	5.7%	0	0	0	0	1	0	0	0	0	
SE	9.0%	9.5%	0	0	0	0	0	0	1	2	1	
SI	5.7%	6.0%	0	0	0	0	1	0	0	0	0	
Total	8.9%	7.7%	1	0	3	4		18	11	12	7	18

We remember that the test was for 91 banks but a bank of a German Land, (Helaba), has refused to participate because sure that it cannot pass the test. The results show that we have 1 German bank with a dangerous ratio under 4%, (In Italy, UK, France0), and this Bank could be the 2nd bank near to default. Then we have in the "grey zone" between 6-7% 6 German banks, 3 in Italy, 2 in France and 1 in the UK. It is clear who is in the most dangerous situation among the top 4 EU-zone economies

And now we focus on the Greek debt.

Chart 28   Greek sovereign exposures by counterparty country

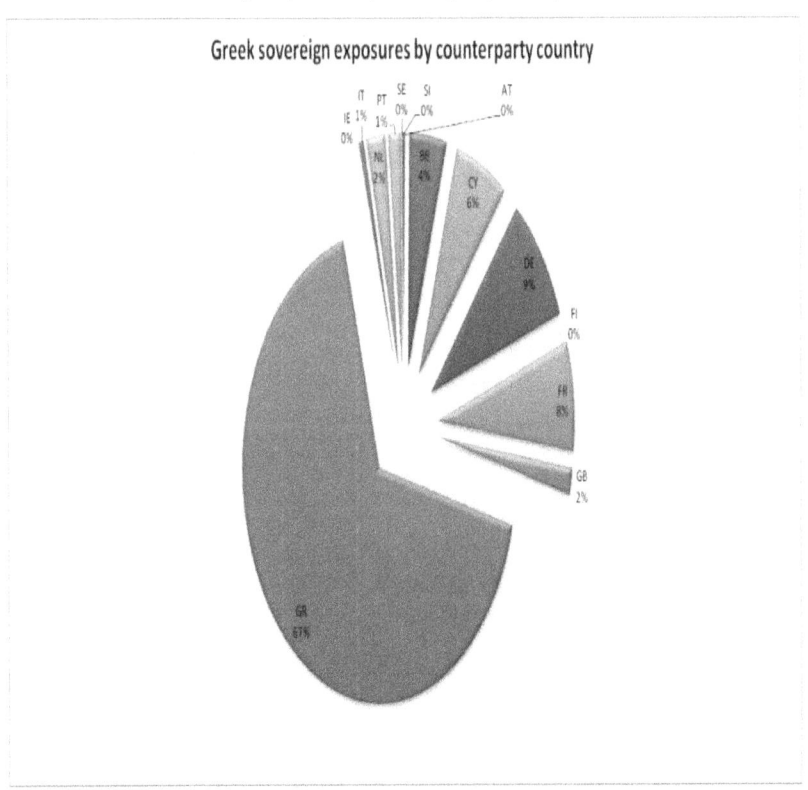

Greek institution exposures by counterparty country

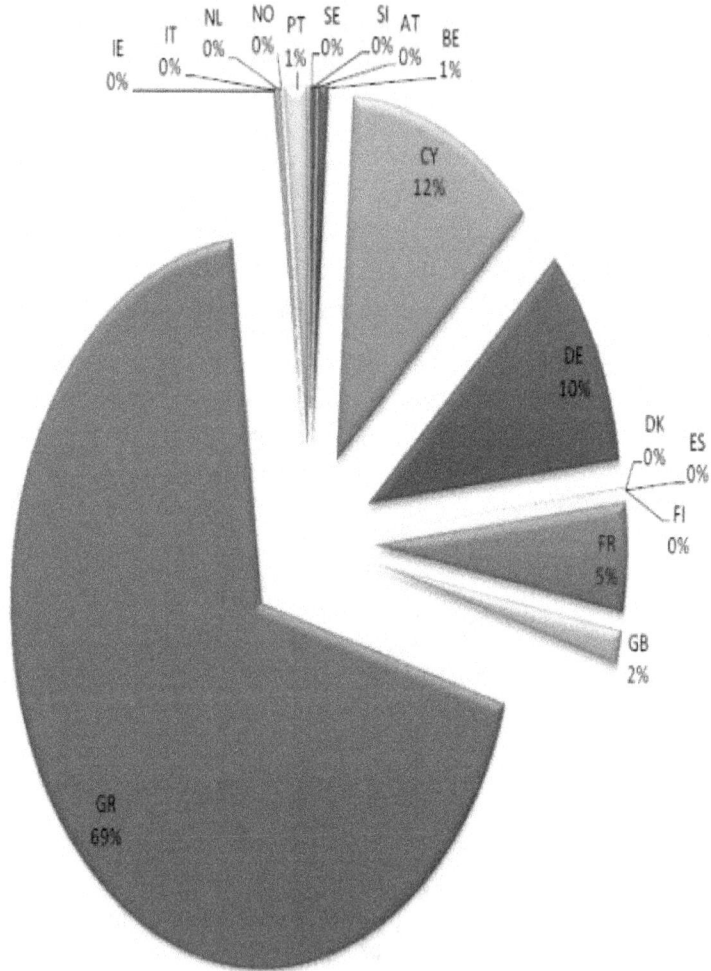

The German exposure is 10%, the French is 5%, the English is 2% and the Italian is 0%.

This shows who has to suffer the most if Greece has a problem and demonstrates that the Greek debt problem is NOT AT ALL an Euro problem in the term that the euro is at the end BUT a an Euro because no one can afford that 2 or

3 important German and French bank can bankrupt more or less at the same time.

This problem is generated because someone has lent the money to Greece.

And why?

Not because, like someone has told in Germany, it was to pay lazy social workers or because the Greeks can retreat before the Germans. Not ...that was lent simply to give to Athens the money to pay infrastructural works, (starting with the Olympics Games), that generate jobs in Germany and France where the product where produced. And not mention of the super-paid carriers of a lot of bankers that lent to Greece the money used to generate profits in a lot of French had German companies. By the way bankers that had these companies as clients and where they sit in the board of directors.

In other words: Athens with the right hand toke the loans and with the left paid companies based in the same countries of the lenders. Logically the governments in Athens are also to blame because these investments were like drug in the economy and they did it to create jobs and electoral consensus as well as to be corrupted by bribes. It was a sad co-responsibility between bankers in Germany and France and politicians in Greece where all could benefit. But for electoral calculations both Chancellor Merkel and President Sarkozy cannot tell that and "punish" important part of their establishments and lobbies. The solution was to blame someone else: Greece.

In German that meant: that not only in Germany only the Germans work and the foreigners not but in also that in Europe the Germans produce and work for all. A strong Germany at the heart of a continent of PIGS. If you read U. Beck and his explication about the German wisdom of their Europe-wide moral superiority you can find interesting element to support this. Or if you read Die Welt you find that the German leadership is wondering why world leaders are wasting time visiting Brussels, London or Paris. They should visit only Berlin to agree about almost anything and then Berlin will call the others to inform and to tell to them what they have to do.

It is not a surprise that this turned on also in diplomatic arrogance.
Without Berlin there is not Europe and either the Europeans work as Berlin wants or there is not Europe.

Again facts and reality from economy and diplomacy proved that this was more a dream than the real case. About diplomacy three events scaled down the supposed and over-credit German power:

a) 2-11-10 France and the UK sign a special military pact cutting-off Germany
b) 12-5-2011 the Visegrad Group, (V4), group of four EU Countries: Poland, Slovakia, Hungary, and Czech Rep. created the first operative European battle group outside both the NATO and the EU. Under the Polish control this military structure in Central Europe has a clear mandate either against Moscow and Berlin.
c) Despite the German wishes both the EU and the NATO went ahead with the intervention under a UN Resolution in Libya.

The last event shows that if there is a place where the European destiny can cross this is Paris and not Berlin. The world meets in Paris when on the table is the European international politics,(Libya),and when there is the euro-problem, (Chancellor Merkel went to Paris and not President Sarkozy to Berlin).

If we talk about the economy we can see that also in this case the supposed German super-power is more supposed than real. We use data issued by the German government, (III)

.- The 1st world market for Germany is France

-Washington is the 4th and Italy is the 5th (only 1 billion Euros smaller)

-China is the 7th market and Austria is the 6th

- Spain is the 11th and the powerhouse Russia is the 13th

-Portugal is the 24th and S. Africa is the 26th, Hong Kong is the 37 .

- In the top 20 world markets we find 12 EU Countries

- if we consider the BRICS their position is : China (7),Russia,(13),Brazil (19), India, (21), S. Africa (26). As term of reference we remember that Belgium is the 8th world market.

 The situation does not change when we consider the top 20 world suppliers for Germany:

- 13 of them are EU countries

- and the Non-EU countries are China(1), USA (3),CH (8),Russia (10), Japan (13), Turkey (17) ,S. Korea (20).

When among the top 20 world German markets we find 12 EU Countries and among the top 20 suppliers we find13 EU Countries it is a bit un-realistic to believe that Germany can leave Europe or that Germany does not need the EU.

Especially if we consider that if Berlin leaves the euro the new Deutsch Mark will re-evaluate not less than 25-30% killing the German export.

These facts supplied by a Governative German source shows how that menace was more based on diplomatic arrogance than on the reality.

Yesterday S&P reduced the Italian rating and in the USA was told that this is the 3end of the EU because Italy is too big, (IV).

Yesterday Chancellor Markel awaked and told that without the Euro the EU cannot survive.

Unlucky it was only yesterday. If she and President Sarkozy told the real situation, (a French and German banking problem), we could avoid the lost of the wealth for millions of Europeans after weeks of wild speculation and, more important, we were not at this point.

But their electoral problems were more important of the European stability and they turned to be populists.

But despite of that Chancellor Merkel has lost an election after the other, (the last in Berlin), and that means that, at least for now, populism and diplomatic arrogance do not pay.

Now she has the chance to use her residual time like a Chancellor like Adenauer and not like a short term minded politicians interested only on preserving electoral power. But, to be honest, Chancellor Merkel, unlucky, is not alone.

Sarkozy, Berlusconi, Zapatero...all were not able to answer to the crisis.All represent the dangerous Crisis of Legitimacy that will create the third phase of this crisis started on 9/15. Unlucky we agree with George Friedman, (V).

Notes

I) 22/7 white Christian fundamentalism

II) European Bank Authority , 2011 EU-wide stress test aggregate report http://stress-test.eba.europa.eu/pdf/EBA_ST_2011_Summary_Report_v6.pdf

III) Außenhandel 2010, 10.03.2011 www.destatis.de

IV) Italy Unsolicited Ratings Lowered To 'A/A-1' On Weaker Growth Prospects, Uncertain Policy Environment; Outlook Negative

V) Crisis of Legitimacy by Dr. George Friedman

Arrogant Capitals: New York and Washington ...
(arrogant for the USA)

October 18, 2011

"But when a long train of abuses and usurpation ,pursuing invariably the same object, evinces a design to reduce them under absolute despotism is their right ,it is their duty, to throw off such government and to provide new guards for their future security" (Thomas Jefferson - "The Declaration of Independence" ,1776)

Yesterday, (I), we have seen how the supposed hot geopolitical American problems in the 2011 are like these in 1992 and that we can easily replace the word China with Japan. We mentioned about the "Great Coalition" ,(where together with the State Actors as created by the Peace of Westphalia sit also Non State Actors), started in the 2008 as ,(also),evolution of that started in the 1972 post-Cold War order as described by President Nixon.

Today we want to deep focus on the internal American situation and on its "Jasmine Revolution". Both the Tea Party and the Occupy Wall Street movements have deep roots in the past. We must not forget why the program to eradicate homeless was created, (and then abused by short term minded CEO´s),after the Million Men March in Washington.

But we have also not forget 4/19 and Oklahoma City.

"Recent reports worry that a major recession could trigger a tidal wave of crime. One segment of the American population that could take advantage of such an opportunity is the so-called patriot movement, an ideology subscribed to by such fanatics as Timothy McVeigh and Terry Nichols -the perpetrators of the Oklahoma City bombing. Found primarily in rural areas, the movement appeals to those who have not shared in the nation´s prosperity ... as society embraces globalization and corporatization.

As the gap between the haves and have-nots continues to wider these disenfranchised citizens may well strike at the government they hold responsible for their misfortune... The militia or patriot movement rose in the 1990s in response to a perception among radical right that the federal government seeks to usurp the Constitutional rights of the American citizens. Based on a ultra-nationalistic, selective populism ... Many of the militia movement´s leaders belong to the Christian Identity religion, which believes that white are the true chosen people of Israel. Identity happens to be the preferred religion for Neo-nazi hate groups . In four years following the Oklahoma City bombing, the FBI has witnessed a significant increase in domestic terrorism.. more than 1.000 domestic-terrorism cases compared to only 100 before the April tragedy. Today s in the past , many economic forces continue to drive the movement ,which has grown to include 435 active groups. Should the economy plunge, these disenfranchised members of society may elect to cast their lot with this demonstrative sector"

It seems something we can read nowadays but it was wrote on 1999 by an NSA , the security company Guardsmark Inc.,(The Lippmann Report 15-8-1999).

This is only one of a mess of historical evidences that tell us that since long time Washington and New York are acting as arrogant capitals frustrating the American politics. We can describe them as a cartel composed by politicians, lobbies and media. This "triangle", since a quarter of century if not 30 years, is saw by a growing number of Americans as a power that has hijacked the nation.

A Gallup Pool found only 19% of American saying they could trust Washington and it was in 1994 !

For most of the Americans lobbyists are groups of parasite central power composed by not less then 200.000 high-income professional. An elite living in a political capital,(Washington DC), that is more and more seen as a rich bipartisan honey pot for the political elected elite. As well the financial and soft power capital,(New York), is seen as an another rich honey pot for the financial, media and banking elites.

At the end and dramatically tow quality capitals, (like Brussels, Beijing, Rome, Paris, Berlin, Madrid ...), completely out of touch with the rest of the country.

President Clinton is quoted to tell in a private interview aboard Air Force One that he wanted to be remembered as the President that restored the chance to live the American Way of Life. It was 1992 and 17 years later another President used the same words with the famous slogan " we can".

It was a President that was talking to a divided country and the key word to describe the relation between elites, (elected and not), and the people was: DISCONNECTION.

As they are still disconnected today it is not a surprise that the Tea Party and the Occupy Wall Street movements are (part of) the answer, from different perspectives, to the same problem.

The synthesis of this more than 30 years old problem can be found in the following points:

I)   Decentralizing/dispersing of power
II) Modifying the US Constitution ´s excessive separation of powers between the executive and legislative branches. (For exp. see the 60 years evolution of the Presidential power of war ,II)
III) Shifting US representative government more toward direct democracy and opening up the 2-parties system
IV) Curbing the role of lobbies
V)   Dismiss the excessive role of lawyers legalism and litigation
VI) Re-mobilizing the national, state, and local governments through updated boundaries and a new fiscal framework
VII) Regulating speculative finance and reduce the Wall St. political power
VIII) Reversing the trend toward greater concentration of wealth and making tax system fairer and more productive
IX) Confronting the power of multinationals minimizing the negative effects of the globalization and magnifying the positive ones.
X)   ) Bringing national and international debt under control

It is easy to tell that this is what Jefferson and the Founding Fathers were scared about and predicated.

Tomorrow we focus on the point VI and about the almost unnoticed not less then50 years old long trend that is been redrawing the North American bounders. Creating a "9 Nations Land". (*)

Notes

I) http://prosumerzen.net/2011/10/17/the-3-
    overlapping-crisis-china-euusa-by-paolo-dealberti/
    t

(*) The mentioned article is published in the forthcoming"Public Governments vs. Private Governments. One year of war between Stata Actors and Non State Actors"

IMF; what if the chief…?

Each person is innocent till is not proven guilty and we respect this pillar of the justice.

For this reason we want to work using a "*what if scenario*" for this article.

Let´s imagine a State Actor that is:

- One of the three leading nations in the EU

-A nation that is a NATO´s pillar as well as a pillar inside the G7,G8 and G20

-A nation that is permanent member of the UN Security Council

-That has the third nuclear arsenal in the world

- That is member of a special club, (a sort of G3 of the military power), because one of the 3 nations in the world either with deep water capability and international power projection capability

- With an international network of alliances

- World leader for the nuclear energy

- With the 2nd best space technology in the world

And now imagine a person that is

- A leading figure in the second party of this nation

- A leading figure of the progressive parties at worldwide level

- A candidate with real chances to win a presidential election

- The chief of the most powerful Functional Organization, (the IMF), in the world. A States Influenced Non State Actor, (SINSA).

- Member of elite clubs around the world

-A person that either belongs to the Bureaucratically Elected Elites, (BTE), an elite elected by the SA´s and to the Politically Elected Elites, (PEE), an elite elected by citizens

And only inside our *"what if scenario"* let´s also imagine that this person is linked to the Trans-national Organized Crime, (TOC), another NSA.

This person has a strong interest for ladies and due to his money and power any Concierge inside a top luxury hotel is a good adviser to find a prostitute. Additionally because resident in a megalopolis and because of this aptitude it is almost more than sure that he has his "private hot directory" of contacts for his *bungabunga* ´s party.

But this is his private life and we are not bigots and we do not comment that.

Till this is something private in his bedroom and the involved subjects are consentient and all is legal we do not see any problem.

Then is totally different if there is a rape and totally different also if this means a structured link with the organized crime.

On clear text the point is only one: how is fragile this person in front of a racket?

It is hard to believe that the TOC did not drill this occasion and once informed about it let all in the hands of some small local gangs specialized on prostitution.

It is more than sure that this escalates till the top level of the TOC and this person become one of their puppet.

It is alarming to see that the intelligence services of two of the biggest and more powerful countries in the world,(France and the USA), as well as the security service of the IMF did not know this situation. A lot of senior officers must supply some embarrassing explications and there is the need, an urgent need, of some clean up.

Again this is a "*what if scenario*" but if this person will be proven guilty this is also an episode that confirms how the relations between the NSA´s and the SA´s are either transversal and above the law.

.And in this case how these relations can be dangerous… .

...

For Geopolitics and more

...

Reconciliation ...

May 17, 2011

Let´s imagine two countries and for now we call them X and Y:

-They share the same language

-They are neighbors

- They do not fight since 90 years

-They had fought 2 world wars and a cold war against the same enemies

-They are part of the same international military alliance

-They share the same international vision and goals as well as alliances

-They are part of the same regional economic and political union

-They have the same commercial law

-They are economically integrated

-Hundred thousands of citizens of Y are born in X and vice versa and still live there

But due to mutual suspicions their Head of States have not visited each other since 90 years.

And for the visit of the Head of State of Y X had deployed the biggest security system in its history,(by the way just last night a terrorist bomb from a local group was found in a place the Head of Y must visit).

But the two people are happy and both the countries describe it as "an historical moment with high political value."

Both use 2 words to synthesize it: **"apologies"**, **„reconciliation."**

Who are them?

Not, sorry, you are wrong … it is not South or North Korea, not the USA and Iran or Cuba, not China and Taiwan, not East and West Cyprus and not Israel and Palestine.

We talk about the United Kingdom and Ireland.

Two countries inside the EU, the NATO, with a common international vision, that fought should-by-should two world wars and a cold war against the totalitarianism …

But despite of that divided by suspicions.

Today the Holy Queen Elisabeth II starts his 4 days official visit, the first since 90 years and during her 60 years of kingdom. **For the reconciliation.** If politics and history need so long time for two countries ,that since the beginning share the same destiny, how can we think to make " nation building" in 12-24 months?

And how can we make such absurd request?

We thank the UK and Ireland for the lesson we are learning.

God save the Queen … and, of course, the President of Ireland!

If the US Army leaves…

May 25, 2011

Premier Netanyahu in his speech yesterday in front of the US Senate told "we defend our self". It is clear that without the massive US economic support the Israel Military Forces, (IMF), cannot do the job alone but the point is other and politically important.

The meaning is: the boots on the fields are ours and you have not to send yours.

This comment was the input for one reflection and one question.

The reflection: the difference between Israel and Europe is that Europe,in the past, alone could not defend itself only with its "own boots". And it is the same today. Logically there was an astonishing difference between the former USSR and the Warsaw Pact military, (both conventional and nuclear), menace against Europe and that of the Arabs countries against Israel. The same today because is always astonishing the difference between the Russian conventional and nuclear menace and that of Syria, Hezbollah and Iran, (even with the bomb). But it also clear that there is another difference: the Europeans could survive under a USSR domination, (as under one Russian), but the Israeli not. President Ahmadinejad has clearly told that if he and his allies win a war the Israeli face a " nazi style final solution". **On other words Israel has been and is been fighting to survive when Europe not.** And anyone supports President Ahmadinejad is supporting a man that wants the same Hitler´s final solution. Not more not less.

The question: what if the US leaves Europe?

We all remember Le Monde title on 10/11/01: "We are all Americans". These days, 10 years ago, we could read it under two perspectives. The first was the total solidarity for the 9/11 tragedy. The second was a lot less noble and a lot more interested because it was simply and only **FEAR**!

Fear to be let alone to face "somewhat run by someone" and, by the way, it was not a coincidence all that talks about the end of Rome.

Did we forget it?

Maybe, "simply", we **want** to forget it. But when we were are talking about the end of Rome we forgot that Rome did not end...Rome survived another 1000 years and its name was Byzantium. When Rome dead Byzantium has token (at least partially) the lead. It is not possible to exactly translate the past into the present to draw the future but let´s to imagine a scenario. Washington starts to act like Byzantium and the scenario is: the US Army leaves Europe to be stationed only in the UK.

A lot of no-global, politicians and intellectuals in Europe, (and not only), will find that a reason for a great party...."*oh.. at the end free from the Yankees and their pro-Zionist policy*!".
We are not among them.

This will be a short party with a sad end ....
Immediately we find that Europe can be targeted by Russians and Iranians missiles.

Not exactly, France and the UK have a card to play and this thank to their capability to implement a nuclear retaliation.

Additionally France and the UK are too far away from the Iranian missiles for the next years.

The first strategic question is: **do Paris and London risk that Marseille and Manchester are annihilate to defend Munich, Barcelona or Firenze against a Russian nuclear attack? Or also, do Paris and London risk a terroristic attack with a weapon of mass destruction against Marseille and Manchester to defend Berlin or Rome or Warsaw against the Iranian menace?**

General De Gaulle answered to such questions and the answer was: not at all!!

It is not by coincidence that France, the UK and Israel started they nuclear programs after the Suez Crisis when Washington,(despite the boring and useless mythology about the Israeli Lobby), where against London, Paris and Tel Aviv.What it will be?

Simply and unlucky tensions will arise between the European regional powers, (the UK, France, Italy, Poland, Germany, Russia, Turkey). And if someone can find it useful only for a novel we kindly remind the meaning of the militarization of Central Europe OUSTIDE the NATO and the EU with the Visegrad Declaration on 12-05-1. That was the creation of the first independent 4-countries-and-run-by-Poland battle group at the hearth of Europe.

All the mentioned countries are classified as "*6 months ahead*". What does it mean?

In 6 months they can have their own nukes because they have all they need for achieving it, (money, technology and the material). For example: Italy with its two small nuclear plants and uranium in its own territory for four state–of-the-art plants for around 70 years can build-up the first 10 nukes in a matter of months. Germany with its nuclear plants,(even if they are all closed tomorrow),can achieve it first 40 nukes in a matter of months. And so on for each EU country with a least a nuclear plant in its territory. A long and deadly list, is it?

No one of these countries can be a regional dominant power but France and the UK together can do it. This will be at the same time a deterrent for any special link between Berlin and Moscow as well a reason to deeper this link, (to be clear Berlin can at any moment buy nukes in Russia to fill-up the gap against London and Paris).

It is only a scenario…something that has not value.

But, maybe, in these days, where too many are so tired of the USA and of the EU, it could be a bit wise also to think about a world without both.

And, logically, some elites will find it interesting for their visions and power, (and to support it as a legitimate trend), as well as others will find it problematic, (and to stop it as a deadly trend).

Our future has multiple options and it is upon to us to choose what we want. Always and we have not alibi if we refuse to choose.
We want a future with both,(the USA and the EU), engaged in a mutual empowerment with all the world.

Asymmetric war?

May 11, 2011

What does it mean?

According to the common meaning it is the case of a war that involves a Not State Actor and a State Actor where the NSA is using not conventional means and strategies. This happens due to its weakness facing a traditional war.

This simply has not a lot of historical sense.

It is told that nothing new is under the sun and it is time that we challenge our ignorance and back to read a bit about history. This kind of wars has been "business as usual" since at least three thousand years and we always called them: **guerrilla.** And since that time it was against pirates or bandits,(please read it as the organized crime of that time and the NSA of that time able to control territories. Do we have forgotten Pompous Magnus? It was more than 2 thousand years ago: Rome Vs. Pirates .What we call today "asymmetric war" is not more and not less that guerrilla in Afghanistan in the XIX as well as in the XXI. But despite of that has a lot of sense to talk about "asymmetric war". It is useful when we talk about how the fighters are fighting. In one ne side the armies under a UN Mandate like the UN Resolution 1973 or the troops in Cot d´Ivoire as well these in Afghanistan are fighting an asymmetric war NOT in the sense that the adversaries are using guerrilla and/or terrorism **BUT in the sense that they act as the armies of a civilized world and self-limit themselves.**

They respect civilians, try to reduce causalities, strike when sure to reduce the collateral effects, respect prisoners and so on. Their enemies?

Look to Libya … and it will be not different anywhere in the world.

One example among others can help us to understand.

The US are discussing about the need of a new kind of smaller nuclear heads to be credible in terms of deterrence. The problem is to avoid overreacting in case of a conventional as well as an "un-conventional", (read a WMD by terrorists), nuke will strike America.

The American nuclear arsenal will annihilate the country that attacked and the US strategists are considering it as **overreacting and having ethic doubts on it.**

Then they have the need to find a different generation of "nukes" able to be a **proportionate** answer.

We are sure that no one of their enemies with a future nuclear capability will have the same respect for the USA. For example, thinking to only to show to the USA how they are vulnerable and then to detonate a bomb in the desert instead of in a metropolitan area.

Not at all, they will kill innocents. This makes a difference and at least for us it has a clear meaning even in a world of "politically correct relativism" like ours. To decide to use a nuke in a desert instead of in a city makes the difference and there is no justification if someone chooses to kill innocents. We have not to change our way and to go ahead on fighting asymmetric wars when it means that we must respect the value of the human life's despite the horror of a war and the BARBARIAN way to act of whom who we face.

… Then

.

In a world lost in its disorder this could be an example of model to imitate. Others can hide behind the **hypocrisy** of an abstention at the UN Council when it is the case of dictators that kills civilians. If we need names it only to remember the last votes about Syria at the UN …

Ankara, Pretoria & the BRICS

April 14, 2011

(Editorial Note: one year later the publication of this article was published inside the prestigious Foreign Affairs: Ruchir Sharma; "Broken BRIC´s" FA Vol. 91 N.6-that That article confirmed this approach as well as all wrote by Paolo Dealberti inside the book "State Actors Vs. Not State Actors")

In these days in China the BRICS are working to „institutionalize" their power.

The G20 is over and this is natural. None could expect more from the G20 and there are not reasons at all to consider it a tragedy. The G20 had only a goal: to find rapid solutions to avoid great depressions. **It was done and its role it is over.**

The world is still (struggling) to search new institutions and/or a new order for the old ones, (a post Breton Woods order).Despite all the triumphalism the BRICS are not at all that.

We hope for them ,(the world needs stability), to have a future more brilliant of the Not-aligned Movement but we consider them not more and not less than a (short/middle term) coalition of interests.

Two of them are yet long time partners: China and Russia, (both members of the Shanghai Group). But to describe the relation between Moscow and Beijing as friendly, engaged and constructive in Central Asia is to be "a bit too much optimist".

The name itself, BRICS instead of BRICT, explains how all is more fragile that we want to credit.

BRICS means Brasil, Russia, India, China and...S like South Africa instead of T like Turkey.

This was a geopolitics mistake. The best solution was BRICST but to include only S. Africa means two things:

a) That at the moment Beijing has the leading role inside the BRICS and to have Pretoria on board answers to its own and exclusive interests in Africa

b) that Ankara is too big, complex and problematic to be "absorbed".

About the real weight of the BIRCS some sample data:

- From a military point of view they cannot do any sustainable action neither in term of projection of power nor to make sure the trade and supply sea lines. Beijing is still totally depending from the goodwill of Washington about its supply lines and its sea line to export. (and it has not a "deep blue waters" navy" but only a power of interdiction thanks to hundreds of Feng anti-ship missiles)

- Economically they are around the 15% of the world trade and the 8% of the world economy ...largely behind the USA

- About the high-end technologies and services the USA have a surplus vs. the world of more than 140 billion US$ and the 5 BRICS are not world leaders but net importers of American high-tech products/services

- About soft power even if the "so called Washington Consensus" is suffering a lot in term of appeal it is hard that they represent an alternative. 18 months ago a Gallup survey among the new Chinese middle class asked them if they want to stay in China or to go to the USA if they can have a choice. The 75% answered that if they can choice they fly to the USA. This middle class it is not only the elite but also the future of China and if 75% of them, despite its privileged status, want to leave the Country, well this should means something or?

- The situation will never be better even if the BRICS will become BRICS+G = Germany,(see the German vote about the UN Resolution 1973).This simply because Berlin cannot solve the weakness of the 5 Countries. Berlin cannot provide international military projection to protect their supply/trading lines and despite its 1st class industry when we talk about "high end" technology also Berlin has a trade deficit with Washington.

- China and India in Iran, Afghanistan, and Central Asia have interests that if not divergent it is hard to describe as convergent

-finally the fight each other to export and all against China

It is to consider them for what they are and can be and to avoid falling in the tramp to give to them too much credit in term of (future and possible but not sure) power.

In a sentence: it is better to avoid over-evaluating them.

In the 80´s each week we heard about forecasts where super Japan was described to be the unchallenged Country leader of the world in the year 2000 and since the ´90´s we see a different scenario.

Could we (at least) suppose that this could be possible also for less structured and solid Countries, (compared with Japan at the top of its power in the ´80s),like Russia, South Africa or China … .

In the long term we consider that Brasil will be the stronger among them, (by the way Brasilia has the best situation about its welfare and pension system among the 5).

But in the short term the most important geo-political consequence is the exclusion of Ankara.

As we wrote Ankara is a reliable partner but also a skilled player aware of its own interests. Under the light of what is going on in Beijing the Turkish decision to support the UN 1973 in Libya and to be a reliable and active NATO member involved in the humanitarian help is assuming all its strategic value.

Ankara has made its decision, (III), at least for the moment..... .

Notes :

(I)   http://prosumerzen.wordpress.com/2011/03/23/turkey-a-skilled-broker-12/

(II)   http://prosumerzen.wordpress.com/2011/03/31/bio-fuel-can-kill-opiumcocainemarijuana/

(III): http://prosumerzen.wordpress.com/2011/03/24/turkey-a-skille-borker-22/

India, Russia and the USA… an example of the USA leading role…

March 14, 2011

If a Country wants to buy weapons before than a producer searches an allied Country. In a sentence: a Government before than a Board of Directors.

The trade of weapons it is always and only a matter between Governments that it is run as business by "private" Companies that usually are ,(more or less), " privately owned national champions",(PONC), and a valuable asset of a Country´s IEP ,(I).

Now let´s imagine that we have two Countries: Alpha (the buyer), and Beta, (the seller).

Let´s imagine that Alpha wants to buy sophisticated weapons like a multirole combat aircraft, a carrier, helicopters, missiles … .

Alpha´s Government will evaluate 3 parameters:

1) Given its budget the best ratio price/quality that this Country can afford to pay, (II)

2) If the seller requires or not political conditions, (for example an end-use monitoring agreement, EUMA. (III))

3) Political, economic "patronage" from the seller, (IV).

At the same time a selling country like Beta has its own 4 parameters to evaluate **because the selling of (sophisticated) weapons it is always more a political than an economic matter,(V):**

(I) the political stability of the Buyer, (VI)

(II) The political reliability of the Buyer, (VII)

(III) How this selling can improve/deteriorate its alliances in the region/worldwide, (VIII)

(IV) The total control of the technology, (IX)

When Alpha finds that Beta fits its parameters and when Beta finds that also Alpha fits its parameters we have the selling.

Now we can translate all into the real world.

If we consider the Buyer´s parameters what do we have?

"Simply" this Country is evaluating a Seller more as "allied / supplier of political and economic patronage" than a seller!

It is interesting to talk about India as buyer and its three biggest sellers: Russia, Israel, and the USA.

Sunil Dasgupta and Stephen P. Cohen, (X), wrote something extremely interesting about the US arms sales for India but they miss this point.

The authors focus on what the US Administration "must do" to conquest India and they forget either that the main political beneficiary and more interested on the venture is India itself. India has more to gain than Washington and it seems that the two authors miss this point.

Let´s consider some elements.

A) Economics: in 2010 India is ranked 15th, (22.043 ML US$), as importing Country for the USA and it is not in the Top 15 World US market. If we read it under an Indian perspective the USA are the 2nd biggest world market for New Delhi, (after Dubai), and two times bigger than China. The USA alone represent for India the 14% of its world market ,(XI).If we consider India as market for the USA we find that Washington is its 3rd world biggest supplier but New Delhi it is not listed among the US 15 Top world markets,(XII). The question is: who needs whom? It seems that New Delhi needs more Washington than the USA India as a market.

B) Politics: it is real that if Pakistan and India have "normal" relations Islamabad can focus more troops and energies against the Taliban. But it is also New Delhi´s interest to avoid a fundamentalist, (as well as a Pakistani-), controlled Afghanistan. On other terms Washington has not to "pray" too much India for an aptitude that allows Pakistan to put at bay the Taliban.That means that we do not need too many "political bargain" to achieve it.

If we keep in mind this we can revaluate and understand what is going on between Russia and the USA.

The day that India can afford to buy Made in USA technology can made a more balanced evaluations of its 3 priorities and that day the choice is for Washington and not for Moscow, (XIII).

This explains who has a better international status: the USA

And if something can, could be learned from this experience is that India it is not the only to take this decision.That "simply" means htat if a country can choose they prefer Washington as "strategic supplier of weapons" instead of Beijing, Berlin or Moscow.

This is a too much under evaluated dimaneion in Washington.And this is sad because it is an extremely important dimension in a world where we tend to overestimate the Chinese or Russian international power as well as the so-called US decline.

Notes:

About the International Economic Power, (IEP), of a Country and the role played by the PONC to see : "Geo-political actors : the SWF an asset more for the SA against the NSA"

(II) Sometime although the quality of the equipment of the selected Supplier lags behind that of other Countries the saving are worth it to the Buyers

(III) A EUMA allows representatives of the selling Country to periodically inspect an inventory transferred to the buying Country in order to verify that the Buyer has not re-sold and/or "transferred" those weapons to a 3rd and not authorized Country . An example. The Country Alpha buys from Beta an anti-tank helicopters with the agreement, (political condition), that cannot sell/lease/"rent" this weapons to a "black listed" third Country, let me say Libya today. But Alpha due to its strategic priorities, (to avoid the slit of in its territory of revolutionary forces based on ethnic affiliation…), and/or economic needs, (the cheaper supply of commodities and/or FDI as well as SWF investment …), "rents" this helicopter to the black listed allied Country. In this case it the Beta´s representative fined it they can suspend either the selling of others helicopters and the supply of spare components as well as the training and this without any payment to the buyer. We have to consider that in a lot of situations those agreements are considered by the Buyer like some kind of limitation of its sovereignty.

(IV) Military agreements , trainings, trading privileges, political support …

(V) Even if we usually talk about long terms contracts for billions US$ or €.

(VI) In this case the risk to consider is that if the buyer is not political stable the selling of a weapon (simply) means to transfer a technology to a Government that someday could be an … enemy

(VII) See note I as example

(VIII) to sell a high-tech jet to India and to refuse it for Pakistan. To sell to Taiwan and the relation with China. To financially support the selling to Poland but not to Bulgaria … and son on…. All are practical examples.

(IX) We have Country like India where it is prohibited to create wholly owned or majority owned subsidiaries in the Country and in this case the concern to "lose" the control of the technology it can be considered too high from a Seller´s point of view.

(X) S. Dasgupta. S.P. Cohen:" Arms sales for India. How military trade could energize US Indian relations" , Foreign Affairs Vol. 90 N. 2 /2011

(XI) Indian Minister of Statistics ,(MOSPI),2010

(XII) The USA sold in India /2010 15.998 ML USD = 2/3 of what Washington sold to Belgium

(XIII) We talk about a market of 100 billion USD$ till 2021. The first test will be the contract for the 126 multi-role combat jets and the competition is among the USA,(F18 Super Hornet and F16),Russia, (Mig 35),France,(Rafale), Germany-Italy-UK,(Eurofighter),Sweden,(Grippen).But even if the USA will lose this contract this has to be evaluate under a normal policy of diversified suppliers as well as a pressure to have more bargain with the USA.

Oil: 2011 like 1971? Not at all

March 11, 2011

The question is if 2011 is like 1971.

Look at what it was on 1971 and what is on 2001:

1971: The oil-producing countries tried to shift the balance of power between themselves and Western oil companies and consumers.

2011: 75 % of the world production is controlled by State Owned Companies, (Petrobas, Aramco...) and an increasing part of their consumers are their internal markets, (rose from 4.8 million barrels a day in 2000 to 7.8 million in 2010 = + 61% in 10 years), and the Asian markets

1971 : the USA pulled out of the Breton Woods system and moved away from the gold standard, effectively devaluing the dollar.Then OPEC, whose oil receipts are denominated in dollars, compensated by raising prices.

2011: we face tensions about the dollar and the yuan but nothing like that in the 1971

Ina sentence:1971 marked the beginning of a new era and 2011 too. But the two situations are different and it does not mean to have a lot of sense to compare them.

Now let's focus on the oil prices:

- 1971 -1980: the increased till the point to be the main source of "stagflation"
- 1981-1985: the price of oil fell from $35 a barrel to $10

- 1990-2000: stabilized at around $20 a barrel for much of the
- 1990s (although it did plunge once again in 1998 to $10).
- 2000-2011: to increase

But oil pricing does not became a "zero-sum game" as too many are (wrongly) supposing.

If we describe it as every rise in prices benefited producers at the cost of consumers, and every reduction in price benefited consumers at the expense of producers we have a "zero-sum game" but in this case we forget a player : **the 3rd (and biggest) beneficiary**.

Who? **Our Governments.**

On average not less than 85% of the price at the gasoline station is tax for the Governments, (it is told that Italy with the tax on oil gains 7 times what the KSA gains with its whole export). And they gain when the price fall as well as when they rise.

We could say that they are the bigger beneficiaries and that then we because those taxes are used to pay the bills of our social infrastructures.

Then focus on demography: from 1971 to 2011 the populations of OPEC countries started to explode, as both life expectancy and fertility rates rose.

BUT with oil revenues falling and populations growing, per capita income began to decline and this is a 30 years trend because the raise of prices cannot compensate that of the population and cannot restore higher level of per capita income.The Governments of the oil producing Countries try to diversify and we have been seeing an international banking and financial center,(Doha), as well as towns of knowledge,(in the KSA), after the other but the crisis debt in Dubai tells us how this it is been working, (by the way Libya among them did not even try to diversify).All tell us that 2011 will be not being like 1971 in term of disruptions.

Why?

I) each new (revolutionary) government will IMMEDIATELY need resources to calm their people and to keep at bay a new revolution = need to sell oil and gas. II) The internal consumption will rise and again this will require to produce and to sell abroad to keep the internal price highly subsided, (something that Iran cannot do because it is a net importer of refined oil).

III) **We have not the USSR anymore**…we tend to forget it and this is a big mistake. In the past the OPEC could play the card of two antagonist blocks. Now we have that its biggest Buyer, (Asia), needs that the rest of the world can absorb its production because it is an "export-oriented" economic bloc. On other terms : if the Producers will racket the West the west will face an economic crisis and then will buy less in Asia and if Asia will less sell will suffer its crisis and ,consequently, will buy less oil… .

The "Oil Shock" weapon does not exist anymore. This is the biggest difference and, at least for that, the 2011 marked the beginning of a new era.

Scenario: The Greater Middle East from Bahrain to Libya

March 9, 2011

If we consider the Greater Middle East Region at the moment among the hottest spots we find Libya and Bahrain.

But before of all we must keep in mind something... what is that?

DE FACTO: the US is YET withdrawn from Iraq!

Yes....it is... if we focus on the remaining (around) 50.000 US troops they are NOT at all a (residual) fighting force BUT training and support personnel with a residual,(even if important), capability in term of self-defense.

In other and more direct terms: **Washington is NOT any more a fighting force in Iraq and this 9 months before the scheduled withdraw**.

Now that we are aware of it back to Libya and Bahrain ...for the 2nd surprise.

Libya and Bahrain have not the same value in London/Paris/Berlin+ Others + Brussels (LPB+O+B), (I), and in Washington.

For **LPB+O+B** counts Libya when for **Washington** counts Bahrain.

Why?

It is a matter of strategic interests,not more not less.

Libya is important for the LPB+O+B for the following strategic reasons:

i. Oil and Gas,(for example Italy imports around 20% of its oil/gas,Germany around the 8,5% making Tripoli its 4th biggest suppliers , (II),)
ii. SWF investments in the so called national business champions ,(III)
iii. illegal immigrants
iv. Political instability across the North Africa and related costs in term of security
v. Other illegal traffics run by the Organized Crime
vi. Relation with business partners in other regions, (for example Spain and its huge business in term of weapons selling to Caracas), as well as in Africa
vii. But if we see them under a Washington-based perspective things are totally different and this means:
viii. Oil and Gas: the USA does not import any oil /gas
ix. The SWF investments in the so called national business champions: no investments in the USA. In this case the only dimension is that we see what happened with FIAT and Lafico
x. Illegal immigrants: the problem does not exist…
xi. Political instability across the North Africa and related costs in term of security: here Washington could have some interests
xii. Other illegal traffics run by the Organized Crime: here Washington could have some interests
xiii. Relation with business partners in other regions: see point b
xiv. Bahrain is important for Washington for the following strategic reasons:
xv. A strategic point where Iran and KSA intersect their regional politics of influence
xvi. Oil & gas: even if the USA has sharply reduced its dependence from the region, (around -30% import in the last 4 years)
xvii. The Greater Middle East : the "vacuum" in Iraq and Afghanistan

xviii. And if we see them under a LPB+O+B perspective:
xix. A strategic point where Iran and KSA intersect their regional politics of influence: it has a value
xx. Oil & gas: high importer, (with the exception of Germany, the UK, France, and Italy)
xxi. The Greater Middle East: the "vacuum" in Iraq and Afghanistan: it has a value

We can find that Bahrain is also important for the LPB+O+B and that more than Libya for Washington.

But before we draw some conclusions we consider important to evaluate a recent comment by Edward Luttwak, (IV). Luttwak told that:

I) The Middle East has not longer any strategic value for the USA
II) About Oil the technology is replacing it faster than we think
III) the Iran bomb...does them really one day has it? (V)
IV) Iran is fast transforming itself in a Post-Islamic Society and the current regime will face troubles

We agree with some of his conclusions and if this is real, and some elements are confirming it, we can see that the USA role as **"pacifier"**, (VI), will be (sharply) reduced in the two extreme of the Greater Middle East region.

And this will affect the whole Europe, (from Lisbon to Moscow and Istanbul), both in term of internal and external stability, (VII).

Let´s start to consider events also under this trend... there is always a lot of possible future...

Notes

(I) We tell LPB+O+B = London/Paris/Berlin+ Others + Brussels and this simply because **the EU does not exist when we talk about a common foreign policy and diplomacy** ... About Libya the "Others" mean Rome for the risk of waves of illegal immigrants with Rome assuming a pivotal role. We can consider that also Madrid could play a role in the case the N. African situation will re-draw the flux of illegal immigrants via Morocco to Spain.
(II) according to the German Armny think-tank Zentrum für Transformation der Bundeswwher Dezernat Zukunftsanalyse: „Peak Oil .Sichereitspolitische Implikationen knapper Resourcen", July 2010

(III) Ian Bremmer, 2009
(IV) Russia Today, 23-2-2011
(V) CIA Report to the Bicameral Security Committee 2004
(VI) as described by Professor J.J. Mearshmeir, 2007
(VII) please do not forget when the EU was let alone to solve the Balkan situation... And let's remember that on 2004 The Head Mufti of Sarajevo, during an interview at "Hard Talk" – BBC, asked to the President Bush Jr. to avoid retreating US soldiers from the Balkan or the war will start again.

Facebook as part of the ordinary life

February 15, 2011

Porsche 911 GT3 R Hybrid :Porsche® has produced a small number of this supercar as a tribute for the account N. 1.000.000 in Facebook® and 1.000.000 names are painted on.

HTC®: has created the 1st smart phone with a dedicated Facebook® button.

This is…superlative brand placement ! We can describe it as mutual marketing where two bands promote each others.

But this is more than that !

This means that now Facebook® is part of us of our quotidian…the revolution has a retroactive dimension .

Since now it is nothing new but our quotidian something we born with and for that…normal .

Business as usual in our ordinary life.

This is positive… and now we wait for the **next** … **"new thing "**

REN: more than the overlaps of art and design

October 6, 2011

REN

why is it interesting to talk about design in a cross-media usually dedicated to geopolitics and to the evolution of the struggles between the SA´s and the NSA´s?

Because design and fashion are the only real universal languages in the term that inside them we find the only common denominator of the world life style. This is important to avoid misunderstandings,(like Fukuyama and Huntington), because one, (and superficial), element is the life style and a different one, (and deep), is the culture.

Culture is the heritage of our history and of the place where we live in our present when life style is a surface that we use for some, (a lot?), of our social interactions and only a small part of it in a long-term process will affect, and modify our culture.

For example you can enjoy oriental meditation music but that does not mean that you will transform yourself cultural habits. Or a lady can sit in a expansive German SUV dressing not less expansive American designers outfits using the state of the art in term of mobile phone devices but if in the KSA that car must be drove by a male. And so on anywhere in the world at any social level.

It is also true that the borderline between design and art is more and more thin, theoretical then real. Global events like " *Fuori dal salone*" in Milano are proving that.

That is positive because if the contemporary art can embody this global code it will be more universal.

Global? …this word raises a lot of negative reactions and this due to two misunderstandings about the so called globalization.

Misunderstanding 1:the globalization did not start with internet or when an American multinational located in an offshore jurisdiction or when the first McDonald opened in China. Not at all. This is "only and simply" the last wave of a multi-secular process.

Misunderstanding2:uniqueness does not mean uniformity.

That means that a uniqueness of style does not mean uniformity in the way they are lived and felt.

REN is a Chinese word and means "caring of others"

REN is also the name of the Beijing International Triennial of Design ,the first in China. We will monitor all the events in our Spiriterial.

Design… a complex world from the crystallization of a social revolution based on the "cult of the brand" originated from that of the ´60´s thanks to IKEA and its "democratic design" to a dynamic borderline where design overlaps with art and vice versa.

It is important to monitor and to understand the code that born there to verify if there is a Chinese soft power. Or, in other terms, if Beijing is able to generate a consensus.

The most the ideas able to reach an international audience and an international appeal are Chinese the most the country is socially vibrant. The more this Triennial is only another platform for others the less Beijing is able to send a global message

<u>Appendices</u>

1- <u>The Power in the XXI</u>

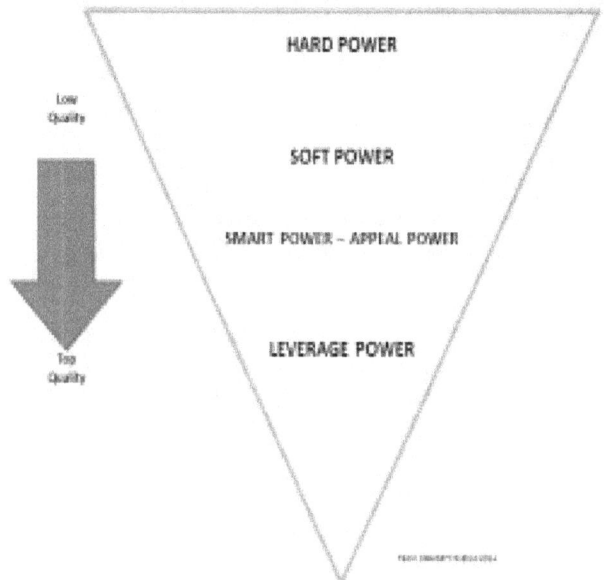

The Hierarcy of Powers

HARD POWER

Low
Quality

SOFT POWER

SMART POWER – APPEAL POWER

Top
Quality

LEVERAGE POWER

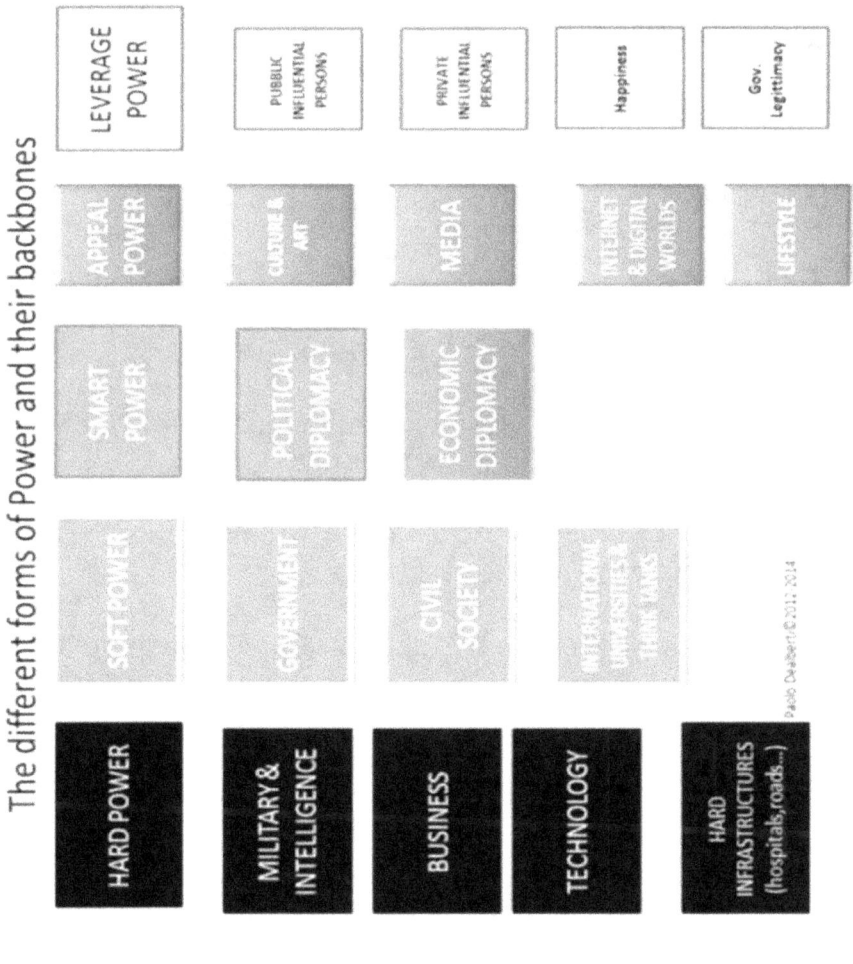

The different forms of Power and their backbones

Who?

The World is composed by 45 Geopolitical Regions including Internet and the Digital Worlds Inside them we have:

-(only) 20 State Actors,(SA´s), with a Full Sovereignty and then SA´s with a Partial Sovereignty, Semi-states, Failed States. (For example from the USA to Somalia)

– 296 leading Towns with at least not less than 296 different as well as equivalent form of modernity

-32 forms of Non Stare Actors,(NSA´s, usually are described only 8 forms but we have found 32)

-3 countries with a Global Projection Capability: the USA, the UK, France

-4 countries with a Nuclear Armeggadon Capability: the USA, the UK, France, Russia

-1 country with Space, Sky, Sea, Land, Cyber, (S3CL),Global Control: the USA

-1 country with an (high-) technology surplus with the whole world: the USA

-a country that will become older before to become rich: China

-Where the 40% of the World is voting this year,(2014)

-And where the ability to decide about the future is NOT considered as an important element of happiness,(people are yet ready to trade-off that with security and products)

-with 5 NSA´s controlling around 95% of the financial in the world,(traded OTC)

– where the USA will stop to import oil and gas from the Middle East in around 6 years from now

-and the National intelligence Agency has forecast,(GT 2015),the born ,(mostly in 3D world based), of a new religion during the year 2015 and that the US Government will fight against US Citizens/Companies due to different geopolitical visions and interests

-where, since 2013, the 3rd most dangerous menace for the US National Security is the Christian fundamentalism and the Israeli Government,(2012), has outlawed as terrorist groups the Jewish fundamentalists

-And… more a lot more…

Where?

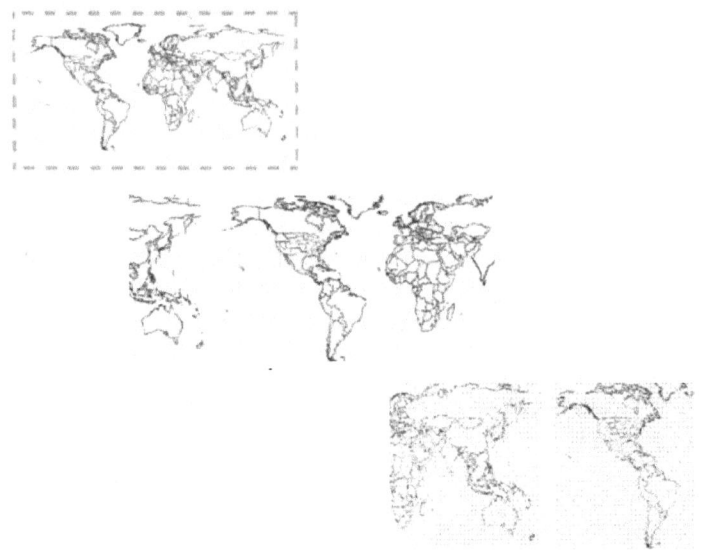

Inside the same world the same planet that we can see using (at least) 3 different world maps:

-The Euro-centric World Map,(Mercatore),and if you are in Europe you are at the center of the World. Then Asia is the East and the Americas are the West. The far eastern town is Samoa Island) and the far western is Nome,(Alaska).

– The Amero-centric World Map and if you are in the Western Hemisphere,(the American continent),you are at the center of the World. Then Asia is the West and Europe is the East. The far eastern town is Bangkok and the far western is Irkutsk,(Russia).

-The Asia-centric World Map, and if you are in Asia you are at the center of the World. Then Europe is the East and the Americas are the West. The far eastern town is London and the far western is New York.

2- The 45 Geopolitical Regions, (including Internet)

I-Recognized Geopolitical Regions

AFRICA

1-Maghreb

Algeria

Lybia

Morocco

Mauritania

Tunisia

2-Sahel

Burkina Faso

Chad

Mali

Niger

3-Western Africa

Capo Verde

Guinea

Gambia

Guinea Bissau

Liberia

Senegal

Sierra Leone

4- Gulf of Guinea

Benin

Ghana

Ivory Coast

Nigeria

Togo

5-Central Africa

Central African Rep.

DRC

Equatorial Guinea

Congo

Cameroon

Gabon

Sao Tome´& Principe

6-Eastern Africa

Burundi

Kenya

Rwanda

Tanzania

Uganda

7-African Horn

Djibouti

Eritrea

Ethiopia

Somali

8-Nile Valley

Egypt

Sudan

South Sudan

9-Sub Tropical Africa

Angola

Malawi

Mozambique

Zambia

Zimbabwe

10-Austral Africa

Botswana

Lesotho

Namibia

S. Africa

Swaziland

11-Indian Ocean

Comoros

La Reunion

Madagascar

Mauritius

Seychelles

WESTERN HEMISPHERE (AMERICAS)

<u>12-Central America</u>

Belize

Costa Rica

Guatemala

Honduras

Nicaragua

Panama

El Salvador

<u>13-Great Antilles</u>

Dominican Rep.

Bahamas

Bermuda

Cayman

Cuba

Haiti

Jamaica

Puerto Rico

Turk & Caicos

<u>14-Little Antilles</u>

Antigua & Bermuda

Barbados

Grenada

St. Kitty & Navis

St. Lucia

St. Vincent & Grenadine

Trinidad & Tobago

<u>15-Atlantic States</u>

Guyana

French Guyana

Suriname

Venezuela

<u>16-Andin America</u>

Bolivia

Colombia

Ecuador

Peru

<u>17-South America</u>

Brazil

Argentina

Chile

Paraguay

Uruguay

<u>18-North America</u>

Canada

Mexico

USA

ASIA

<u>19- Indian Subcontinent</u>

Bangladesh

Bhutan

India

Maldives

Nepal

Sri-Lanka

20-South East Asia

Cambodia

Laos

Myanmar

Thailand

Vietnam

21-South West Asia

Indonesia

Brunei

Malaysia

Philippines

Singapore

22- North West Asia

China

Japan

N. Korea

Mongolia

S. Korea

Taiwan R.o.C.

EUROPE

<u>23-Central West Europe</u>

Austria

Germany

Liechtenstein

Switzerland

<u>24-Netherlands</u>

Belgium

Holland

Luxembourg

<u>25- Northern Europe</u>

Denmark

Finland

Greenland

Iceland

Norway

Sweden

26-British Islands

Ireland

UK

27-Southern Europe

Andorra

France

Italy

Monaco

Portugal

San Marino

Spain

Vatican

28- Central Western Mediterranean

Cyprus

Greece

Malta

Turkey

29-Balkans

Albania

Bosnia-Herzegovina

Kossovo

Bulgaria

Croatia

Macedonia

Serbia

Romania

Slovenia

30-The Baltics

Estonia

Latvia

Lithuania

31- Eastern Europa

Bielorussia

Moldavia

Russia

Ukraine

32-Central Europe

Czech R.

Poland

Slovakia

Hungary

MIDDLE EAST

33- Middle East

Palestina

Jordan

Irak

Israel

Siria

34-Arabic Peninsula

KSA

Kuwait

Oman

Qatar

UAE

Yemen

CENTRAL ASIA

<u>35-Central Western Asia</u>

Afganistan

Iran

Pakistan

<u>36-Caucasus</u>

Armenia

Azerbaijan

Georgia

<u>37-Central Asia</u>

Kazakhstan

Kyrgystan

Tajikistan

Turkmenistan

Uzbekistan

OCEANIA

38-Oceania

Australia

Fidji

Kiribati

Marshall

Micronesia Fed. States

Nauru

New Zeland

French Non Indeppendent Terr.

Palau

Papua New Guinea

Samoa

Slomon Isl.

Tonga

Tuvalu

Vanatu

II- UNRECOGNIZED Geopolitical Regions

39-The Great North

USA

Canada

Russia

Greenland

Norway

40-The Great South

USA

New Zealand

Chile

Russia

Australia

Green Peace (Freehold?)

Japan

France

Denmark

Italy

UK

Argentina

Finland

Poland

China

North Korea

Brazil

Sweden

41-Internet (Free Access & Censored Access)

Google

Bing

Yahoo

WordPress

FaceBook

Utube

Twitter

Linkedin

Ted

The Dark Internet

42-Virtual World Cultures (Proto-States of DUAL Citizenship)

SecondLife

IMVU

Entropia

43-Freehold

? Freedomship ??

? Private State with a Reduced Sovereignty ??? For example: the 17 Private Towns (from Portugal to the K.S.A.) ?? The next step for the more than 20.000 Gated Communities worldwide ?

III – The "NEW" recognized Geo-politic Regions

44- The Greater Middle East

Afghanistan

Algeria

Armenia

Azerbaijan

Burkina Faso

Burkina Faso

Capo Verde

Chad

Chad

Djibouti

Egypt

Eritrea

Ethiopia

Gambia

Georgia

Guinea

Guinea Bissau

Irak

Iran

Israel

Jordan

Kazakhstan

KSA

Kuwait

Kyrgyzstan

Liberia

Lybia

Mali

Mauritania

Morocco

Niger

Niger

Oman

Pakistan

Palestine

Qatar

Senegal

Sierra Leone

Syria

Somali

South Sudan

Sudan

Tajikistan

Tunisia

Turkmenistan

UAE

Uzbekistan

Yemen

45- The Indo-Pacific Corridor

India

Malaysia

Indonesia

Sri-Lanka

Australia

Papau-New Guinea

3- The 296 Leading Towns

2nd Life

Abuja

Acapulco

Accra

Addis Abebha

Aden

Alba

Alchi

Algeri

Alma-Ata (Almaty)

Amman

Amsterdam

Anchorage

Andorra la Vella

Ankara

Antananarivo

Athens

Atlanta

Auckland

Baargaal /Pir

Baghdad

Baku

Baltimore

Bangalore

Banghkok

Banjul

Barcelona

Basseterre

Beirut

Belmopan

Berlin

Bern

Birmingham

Bollywood

Brasilia

Bridgeport

Bridgetown

Brunswick

Brussels

Bucarest

Budapest

Buenos Aires

Busan

Butyaalo /Pir

Caiman Isl.

Cairo

Calexico

Camberra

Cambridge (USA)

Campione

Cape Town

Castries

Charlotte Amalie

Chicago

Ciduad Juarez C

Cleveland

Colima

Conakry

Copenhagen

Daegu

Dakar

Dallas

Damascus

Davenport

Daytona Beach

Denver

Denver

Des Moines

Detroit

Dhaka

Doha

Dubai

Dublin

Durango

Eastport

Eureka

Evansville

Eyl /Pir

Fairbanks

Fort Myers

Fort Pierce Station

Fort Wayne

Frankfurt

Fresno

Fukuoka

Garacad

Gaza

Geneva

Geneve

Georgetown

Gibaltar

Grand Turk

Guadalajara

Guatemala City

Guernsey

Guerrero

Hajjah Sanaa

Hamburg

Hamilton

Hanoi

Harare

Hartford

Helsinki

Hobyo

Hong Kong

Honolulu

Houston

Huntsville

Ibiza

IMVU

Indianapolis

Ingostadt

Islamabad

Isle of Man

Istanbul

Izmir

Jacksonville

Jakarta

Jalisco H/M

Jersey

Johannesburg

Kampala

Kiev

Kigali

Kingston

Kingstown

Kinshasa

Kodiak

Krakow

Kuala-Lampur

Lahej

Leeds

Lille

Lisbon

Little Rock

Ljubljana

London

Los Angeles

Los Angeles/ Long Beach

Louisville

Luanda

Luxembourg

Lyon

Madeira

Madrid

Managua

Manama

Manchester

Manila

Mayorca

Mecca

Medellin

Melbourne

Memphis

Mexico City

Miami

Michoacan H/C

Milano

Minneapolis

Mobile

Mogadishu

Monaco (Princ. De)

Monterey

Montevideo

Montreal

Moscow

München

Naco

Nairobi

Napoli

Nassau

Neuvo Leon/c&e

New Dheli

New Haven

New London

New York

Niamey

Nicosia

Nogales

Oaxaca H

Ocala

Oranjestad

Orlando

Osaka

Oslo

Ottawa

Palermo

Palm Springs

Panama City

Paris

Peking

Pensacola

Peoria

Peshwar

Philadelphia

Phoenix

Pittsburgh

Port Canaveral

Port Everglades

Port Hueneme

Port Manatee

Portland

Prague

Pretoria

Puebla

Quad-Cities

Rabat

Ranstad

Rhine-Ruhr

Riga

Riga

Rimini

Rio de Janeiro

Rockford

Roma

Ryhad

Sa´dah

Saint George

Saint Martin

Salt Lake City

San Diego

San Francisco

San Francisco

San Jose

San Juan

San Luis

San Marino

Sanford

Santiago

Santo Domingo

Sao Paulo do Brasil

Savannah

Seattle

Seoul

Shangai

Silycon Valley

Sinaloa

Singapor

St. Louis

St. Petersburg

Stockholm

Stuggart

Sydney

Taipei

Tallin

Tamaulipas

Tampa

Tampa Bay

Tashkent

Tehran

Tel Aviv

The Valley

Tijuana

Tirana

Tokyo

Torino

Toronto

Trenton

Treviso

Tucson

TunisiUlan Bator

Vaduz

Valdez

Valencia

Valletta

Vancouver

Varna

Vaticano

Veracruz E

Victorville

Vienna

Warsaw

Washington

West Palm Beach

Willmestad

Wellington

Wilmington

Xarardheere /Pir

Yaounde

Zagreb

Zinjibar

Zurich

4- The 32 families of Not State Actors,(NSA´s)

Benign Organizations,(BO)

Functional Organizations, (FO)

Global Media Outlets ,(GMO)

Holistic Movements,(HM)

Influential Advising Company,(IAC)

Influential Advising Entities,(IAE)

International Organizations,(IO)

Militias Forces,(MF)

Civil Societies Political Organizations,(COPO), (not the Political Parties)

Multinationals ,(MNC),

National Industrial Champion,(NIC),

National International Economic Powerhouse, (NIEP),

National Liberation Movements (NLM)

Non Governative Organizations (NGO)

Transanational Organized Crime, (TOC)

Politically Structured Cyber-Virtual Worlds , (PSCVW)

Private Controller ,(PC)

Private Powerful People,(PPP)

Private Government Powerhouse,(PGP)

Private International Financial Powerhouse,(PIFP)

Private Security Forces, (PSF)

Private State Powerhouse,(PSP)

Privatized Functional Organization,(PFO)

Regional Organizations, (RO)

Political Elected Elites,(PEE)

National & International Governmental Bureaucracy,(N-IGB)

States Within Failed States,(SWFS)

States Within Nations-States,(SWNS)

Terroristic Groups ,(TG)

The Super NSA, (SUNSA)

Towns Within Failed States, (TWFS)

Towns Within Nation States, (TWNS)

5- The State Actors,(SA´s)

Here are listed 181 State Actors according to their level of stability.

1- Super Stable

Finland
Sweden
Denmark
New Zealand
Luxembourg
Iceland
Ireland
Australia
Canada
Germany
Switzerland
Norway
Austria
Netherlands
Monaco
Vatican City

2- Stable

Belgium
Slovenia
United Kingdom
United States
Singapore
South Korea
Japan
Uruguay
Czech Republic
Poland
Chile
Malta
Lithuania

Spain
Mauritius
Italy
Argentina
Qatar
United Arab Emirates
Hungary
Latvia
Costa Rica
France
Portugal
Estonia
Slovakia

3-Low Instability

Greece
Barbados
Oman
Croatia
Montenegro
Bahamas
Bulgaria
Panama
Romania
Mongolia
Antigua & Barbuda
Kuwait

4-Medium Instability

Brazil
Trinidad
Bahrain
Brunei
Grenada
Albania
Jamaica
Ukraine
Malaysia
Cyprus
Belize
South Africa
Macedonia
Samoa
Ghana
Kazakhstan
Seychelles
Botswana

5- High Instability

Azerbaijan
Indonesia
Turkmenistan
Belarus
Bosnia
Moldova
Tunisia
Dominican Republic
El Salvador
Mexico
Vietnam
Micronesia
Gabon
Cuba
Saudi Arabia
Peru

Paraguay
Armenia
Suriname
Guyana
Namibia
Lesotho
Nicaragua
Algeria
Ecuador
Honduras
Benin
India
Russia
Turkey
Jordan
Maldives
Venezuela
Thailand
Sao Tome
Serbia
Morocco
Cape Verde

6- Very High Instability

Guatemala
China
Tanzania
Senegal
Madagascar
Laos
Colombia
Comoros
Georgia
Libya

Papua New Guinea
Djibouti
Swaziland
Kyrgyzstan
Equatorial Guinea
Lebanon
Zambia
Uzbekistan
Angola
Togo
Cambodia
Malawi
Iran
Congo (Republic)
Israel
Palestine (West Bank-Gaza)
Fiji
Bolivia
Gambia
Bhutan
Mozambique
Philippines
Tajikistan
Solomon Islands
Mali
Rwanda

7- Extremely High Instability

North Korea
Liberia
Kenya
Niger
Ethiopia
Burundi
Syria
Uganda
Eritrea
Myanmar

Cameroon
Sri Lanka
Bangladesh
Nepal
Mauritania
Timor-Leste
Sierra Leone
Egypt
Burkina Faso

8- Dangerous Instability

Central African Republic
Haiti
Afghanistan
Yemen
Chad
Guinea Bissau
Guinea
Pakistan
Cote d'Ivoire
Nigeria
Zimbabwe

9- Civil War (Explosive Instability)

Afghanistan
Somalia
Congo (D. R.)
South Sudan
Sudan
Iraq

Books published by the Author with JEWIR.

Paolo Dealberti´s books are all cataloged by the Library of the Congress of the United States of America.

Novels : (La Saga degli Speculari)

  I. Etnia Avatar
 II. Obiettivo: Fermare Obama

To be puslished:

III. Humanpolitics
IV. Grecia: debito 2.0
 V. Utopia Reale

International Politics and Economy:

  I. Governi Pubblici Vs. Governi Non Statali. La vera
      guerra che attraversa il mondo
 II. Legittimacy
III. State Actors Vs. Not State Actors

To be published:

IV. Italia Responsabilita´1.0
 V. Ak47: Noi Vs Noi,(vincere contro il terrorismo e
     perdere contro il terrore)
VI. Zenprosumer, lifestyle 2.0

You can follow Paolo Dealberti at:

www.appealpower.com